THAT TIME I LOST MY MIND

A MEMOIR ABOUT LOSING YOUR MIND ON A
VIPASSANA RETREAT BUT ALSO WORMS,
INFERTILITY, BUDDHISM, BROOMING AND
EVERYTHING ELSE, MORE OR LESS.

ADAM FLETCHER

Copyright © 2023 by Adam Fletcher

All rights reserved.

No part of this book may be reproduced in any form or by any electronic or mechanical means, including information storage and retrieval systems, without written permission from the author, except for the use of brief quotations in a book review.

"When there is nothing left to burn, you have to set yourself on fire."

Stars, Your Ex-Lover Is Dead

* * *

Dedicated to all those I defriended along the way; sorry I wasn't better.

1

Badneudorf*, Germany, 2019

Something in my mind had snapped. I grabbed the top of the fence and hoisted my leg over. They'd said there were no fences here. That this wasn't a prison.

They'd lied.

Coming here was a bad idea. Her idea. I wasn't strong enough for this place. Wouldn't make it to the end, even if our relationship was at stake.

I looked out at the empty fields on the other side of the fence and there, in the distance, that small provincial town. A place where there would be normal life, normal people, normal cheeseburgers.

GIN AND TONIC.

I swung my other leg over, so I was sitting on the narrow wooden fence, which wobbled beneath me. It was only a small drop to freedom. Once down, I'd be able to run, something else they'd banned here; they'd banned everything here.

Was I really going to do this?

Yes.

Wait, was that a whistle? I turned back to the camp. It was him. YoungUriGellar. He was walking towards me wearing that same wide, unhinged grin they all wore.

"Come down," he said, and then, to my surprise, dropped the grin. "I have bad news."

*I forgot to write down the name of the town, but all rural German towns have Bad and Neu in their names, so there's about a 50 percent chance it was called Badneudorf, and even if it wasn't, it wanted to be.

2

> Evelyn: Where are you?
>
> Adam: Office.
>
> Evelyn: It's Saturday.
>
> Adam: Deadline.
>
> Evelyn: You set your own deadlines.
>
> Adam: I'm a hard taskmaster?
>
> Evelyn: Come home. I have a surprise.

I sat up and snapped my laptop shut. I was on the black leather couch in my office watching a thrilling documentary about activists in Scotland fighting the development of a golf course. Heroes. It was indeed Saturday, but that was no excuse to not use this place as an excuse to not be at the home I shared with my girlfriend, Evelyn, a woman who had once been perfect and, I hoped, might become it again.

Lately, I came here to get away from her.

Why would she tell me about a surprise? Why would

she surprise me in the first place? She knew I hated surprises. It couldn't be... could it? I turned the pages of my mental calendar. No. We were still three or four days away. And she kept saying how normal she felt, but then she'd become so enormously pessimistic — she was her own personal rain cloud. Our lives had become very damp.

I went out to the street and climbed onto my bike. Ten minutes and three almost-collisions with SUVs later, I opened the grey door to our building and trudged up the stairs.

First floor.

Second floor.

Third floor.

Didn't this usually take longer? Why were there so few stairs suddenly? Had someone removed stairs? Usually I wished for fewer stairs; not anymore.

Fourth floor.

Our door. I took out my phone, scrolled around, put my phone in my pocket, sighed, considered going back down and then coming back up even more slowly. Maybe on my stomach. What kind of mood would she be in? It was impossible to say, but it would be somewhere on the scale between quiet despair and... very loud despair.

I opened the door. "Hey," I shouted down the hallway.

"Hi," she said, emerging from the kitchen into the hallway, unruly blonde hair in a loose ponytail. She was wearing a blue knitted jumper and fluffy white slippers and holding a red coffee cup in two hands, looking as if she were in an advert for chamomile tea. She was at war with her body and no longer treated it to nice things, just baggy things. At her feet and bulging was my Adidas sports holdall. The holdall that usually lived in the bottom of our wardrobe.

Why is that there? Is she kicking me out? Do I want to be kicked out? Is that feeling... relief?

Wait. Next to the bag. Rolled up and red. A cushion? Two cushions? A yoga mat? I didn't own a yoga mat. Yoga was just synchronised bending; I hated bending.

"Going on a trip?" I asked, nodding towards the bag while feigning nonchalance, a skill for which I had both practice and natural aptitude.

She blinked slowly. "It's *your* bag, Sherlock."

"Oh... right."

"*You're* going on a trip." She smiled mischievously with a bounce of her thin eyebrows. "But we need to talk first. Couch?"

I turned towards the living room door. "O-kay?"

She followed me to our vintage white three-seater sofa. We'd found it together, in a junk shop pretending to be an antique shop, just after I'd moved in two years ago. Back then, we'd spent so many nights curled up on it, music wafting from background speakers, making out and telling stories and gulping wine and eating whatever she'd cooked that day. I gained five kilograms in five months.

These days, it was mostly my couch alone. She preferred the red one on the next wall. The low, rectangular Scandinavian coffee table between the couches was bare except for a stack of highlighted, sticky-noted journal articles. She'd been doing her frenzied late-night reading again, dropping down rabbit holes, emerging with new reasons to doubt.

I sat nearest the wall while she took the place nearest the door. The middle seat was empty; no-man's-land. I looked up at the feature wall we'd painted mauve. Hanging on it was a framed picture of us in Winnie, the tuk-tuk we'd raced together in India just after we'd met. She was driving, and I was hanging out the side hoisting a selfie stick.

The first flush of our relationship; a time before we'd even known there would be a relationship. I didn't recognise us. That year had been a golden one — the tuk-tuk race, three intense months in Turkey, moving in together, several more adventures in Thailand and Sri Lanka, and through it all, our love was light, pure, unsullied. A story we were in control of, each chapter better than the last.

On the other side of the room, her dull, striped Turkish rug and my beautiful, ornate Iranian rug clashed and bickered like an old married couple who wished to be neither. Why had we tried to smash two perfectly good living rooms together into this one cluttered clash of cultures? The candle at the centre of the table had been the same height for months. When did we last host? If I didn't want to be here, why would anyone else?

She put down her cup on the coffee table. "So," she said, turning inwards, drawing up her legs, shuffling back, propping herself up with several cushions and the firm arm of the sofa, knees to her chest. A defensive posture in what was likely to become a fractious war of words. I felt as though I'd been dipped in bees. They were swarming, stinging my throat closed. Was this it? Was this really the end?

I crossed my arms. Opened my arms. Crossed them again. "You're not coping with this well," she said, not needing to say what the *this* was. The *this* dominated our lives. Or, more precisely, our increasingly invasive attempts to reverse it.

"Me?" I spluttered. "I'm coping fine. It's you who's struggling."

"No," she said, steeling herself, blinking away a tear. Why? I'd seen her cry so much over the past months it no longer moved me. It was like weather, rolling in and out.

"You aren't doing the work," she said.

"We've done the work. They said it was picture perfect this time. It's *going* to work. Have a little faith." I tweaked my hips in homage to George Michael.

"It's not going to work. We needed to do the ultra-long, but no one would let me."

"It's too early to know."

She took a deep, resigned breath. "No, it's not. Look, do you remember a month ago when we found that flyer at the clinic? Vipassana," she said, the word like a bullet fired from a gun. "I wrote them that day because I knew you wouldn't."

I remembered. A ten-day silent retreat that promised to free my mind and make my soul soar on the breeze of inner insight.

My eyes became thin slits. "You're a sneaky person, you know that?"

She shrugged. "Maybe. Only two cycles left after this one fails. You need to think about what happens after that."

"Things go back to how they used to be?" I said, my voice rising. "We have fun again? Like the old days? The fun days? You remember the fun days, right?"

"We might be post-fun."

"How will Vipassana help with that? It's you who's lost your humour, not me."

"Humour might be part of the problem."

"Humour is never the problem."

"It's a shield. And since you won't do therapy with me. Or alone." She shook her head as if the stupidity of this still stung. As if she were the one swarmed by the bees. "This will have to do. It's too much time not to learn something about yourself. About us. If there will be an us."

"THERE WILL BE AN US."

"Your train leaves in an hour," she said.

"What?" I went cross-eyed. "No. Why?"

"I tried to book it for later in the year. For after... you know." I knew. "But it's always full. Apparently, people try for years to get a spot. They called me this morning. There was a cancellation. Who can find a spare eleven days on such short notice?" She chuckled. "Only you."

"I don't care about meditation, though. It's just sitting with closed eyes but not being allowed to sleep."

"It's not about the meditation."

My gaze darted around the room. "But if I were going to do it, which I'm not, because it's stupid, I'd need time to prepare and I mean, in like four days we'll know, right?"

She thumbed her ear. "It hasn't worked. It never works. How long have we been trying already?"

"Don't say the number."

"And even *if*," she said, rolling her eyes at the impossibility of that, "and you find out a few days later, that's not a big problem, right?"

"I suppose not, no."

"It's not how I would have wanted it, but none of this is really, is it?"

I tugged at the hairs on my forearm. "I can sit in silence for ten days, but I won't learn anything."

"You will. If you make it. A lot of people quit."

"I wouldn't quit. I guess why this would hard for other people, but it won't be for me. But anyway, I can't afford it. The last year has been ruinously expensive."

"It's free," she said. "Well, pay what you want."

My mouth slackened. "Why would they offer it for free?"

"I guess they really believe in it?"

"The fools."

We sat in silence, sizing each other up, refusing to break eye contact. It felt like the end of a poker hand, when you're sure you know what the other person is holding but have to decide how much you're willing to bet on what you think you know. I really didn't want to go, but then I also didn't want to be here. And I didn't like that she thought I wouldn't make it. I wanted to prove her wrong. To spite her. "I need time to prepare."

"Why would you need to prepare for something that you can do so easily?" she countered.

"Hmmm."

"And I just found out myself. And you were out, somewhere, as usual."

A small thunderbolt of guilt hit me.

"And I had to buy meditation cushions," she said.

"Do you really think I can't sit in a room alone for ten days?"

"Does it matter what I think?"

"About me?" I frowned. "Yes."

"No. I don't think you can sit in a room alone for ten days. Not without writing, anyway."

"Am I allowed to write?"

"No."

"Shit."

She shrugged. "Yeah."

"I'm at peace," I said. "My mind doesn't attack me like yours does."

"It does," she said. "Just differently. We lost control of this, somehow." The *this* again. "I'm trying to understand why. I need you to do the same, okay? This is where you can do that. This will make you do that."

"I'm mined. My books are my therapy."

"No," she said. "God, sometimes I feel like I know you better than you know yourself."

I laughed, or tried to, but managed only a snort. "That's a bold statement."

"You have a lot to think about," she said.

"We still have options." I reached for her hand, but she didn't offer it.

"Not really," she said. "I'm sorry this is now, but it's worth doing anyway. Do it. *Please.*"

I broke eye contact and looked out the window at the building opposite. A couple there had recently had a child and was rocking it before their large window, lips moving.

"Fifty minutes," she said. "Your train."

"Fuck."

"Yeah."

3

After a madcap, cushion-dragging dash, I collapsed into the train seat. A whistle sounded and soon, the city faded away like a bad modernity dream, replaced by what Germany did best — flat brown agricultural fields. To spice things up, it threw in a single grass-munching cow. When it wanted to go really wild, it put that cow on a small hill.

I slipped on my large black headphones and blasted Kate Bush for the feels, settling in for the ride. Some people might have been anxious about what I'd just agreed to do — especially if their significant others were convinced it was going to be intense and challenging — but I was mostly just happy to have eleven days to myself. Eleven days in which I wouldn't have to sit in the wreckage of our relationship. I felt as if I'd been let out of prison and then handed a ticket to go on holiday. It wasn't all-expenses paid but the next best thing: pay what you want.

I wanted to pay very little.

What Evelyn had done was odd but not out of character. After all, she'd invited me to India on a whim, a night after we'd first met. She'd whisked us off to Istanbul for three months soon after we got back. She was impulsive, and I liked that about her. And this was a kind of holiday too, wasn't it? Except I was going to journey deep inside my mind, a destination I loved.

I know you better than you know yourself. That doozy of a sentence kept me entertained for the whole four-hour train ride. I'd lived for thirty-six years inside the fortress of my mind. How could someone who'd visited only its manicured front lawn know what beliefs, delusions, traumas, dreams, quirks, and neuroses I kept behind its high, guarded walls?

Many sad cows later, the train deposited me in a disgustingly average rural German town: a windy, unheated train station, two discount bakeries (opposite and, I suppose, also at war with each other), a wilting flower shop, a Greek restaurant, and light rain splattering immaculately paved roads whizzed over by young cars driven by old people. It could have been any town in Germany. A woman knocked into me with her cushions as she darted towards a dirt-speckled minibus. It was the only vehicle in the train station's car park. What was her rush, I wondered, before remembering that she *wanted* this. She was eager to learn Vipassana, eager to free her mind of its mental bondage.

I followed her.

The drive to the retreat centre took only a few minutes on empty roads that cut through rolling, grassy hills. The centre was shaped like a capital I. At one end, a new two-storey mediation hall, at the other, the canteen with a large back terrace. The middle was a series of four single-storey, red-brick buildings set next to a sweeping, forested vista stretching down to a nearby farm. It was basic, but immaculately clean. It looked like a place where celebrities paid a lot of money to drink kale smoothies while battling stubborn demons. Only I wasn't a celebrity. I was going to pay what I wanted, and I didn't have any demons.

A thin red rope strung at waist height divided the paved walkway into two. A sign guided women to the right side, towards their own entrance, and men to the left towards ours. The whole retreat would work like this, the genders strictly separated. Why though? Did they really think I couldn't meditate near a woman? That I'd become so aroused by the sight of her shapely lady bottom in loose-fitting yoga pants that I'd be pushed from the path to enlightenment?

I mean, they should have had a bit more faith in us.

A skip in my step, I followed the rope and put my bag on the pile outside the building's entrance, smiling to myself, happy to be away. I went inside and took a pamphlet from the table before joining the back of a long queue; the worst kind of queue. The room was bright. Light streamed in from wide sliding glass doors that led out to a substantial patio. The walls were painted orange. It smelt of cleaning products laced with lemon. Few people were talking. I was happily reading my pamphlet when the man behind me cleared his throat theatrically.

I ignored him.

"Ha," he said.

I kept ignoring him.

He chuckled. Then chuckled again. "Hahaha."

I turned around a tiny bit. He was a heavily bearded ginger bear of a man with wonderful, piercing, slightly crossed green eyes. He was moving from side to side and had a ragged edge to him, as if he'd just fallen out of a tree and might be concussed. Despite appearing to be a fully sized adult, he was wearing denim dungarees, one side unbuttoned, over a red long-sleeve T-shirt.

"First time?" he asked.

"Yeah."

He chuckled again. "You can always tell the first timers. They don't look scared."

"How many times have you done it, then?"

"This is my fifth Vipassana."

I shrugged. "Can't be too hard then, can it?"

"You'll see," he said, ominously.

"Okay," I said, and turned around to return to my pamphlet.

Vipassana is one of India's most ancient meditation techniques. Long lost to humanity, it was rediscovered by the Buddha more than 2500 years ago. The word Vipassana *means "seeing things as they really are". It is the process of self-purification by self-observation.*

Was I impure? I wondered, as I whistled Kate Bush's eighties-drenched timeless masterpiece *Running Up That Hill*. As I did, I could feel the heat of this shaggy man-bear's gaze warming the back of my head, willing me to turn around and engage him. But I didn't need advice. This wouldn't be hard; it was just going to be boring.

"Yes," he said, into the air. "Huh."

I ignored him some more.

"Good leaflet?" he asked.

I turned slowly, making a real show of it. "Hmm?"

"I remember my first time," he said.

"Oh, yeah?"

He rocked back on his heels as his eyes rolled upwards. "Hell."

"It's not a very good leaflet, no."

One begins by observing the natural breath to concentrate the mind. With a sharpened awareness, one proceeds to observe the changing nature of body and mind and experi-

ences the universal truths of impermanence, suffering, and egolessness.

I liked my ego just fine. "I nearly didn't make it, to be honest with you," he continued, after no encouragement at all. "Yeah, it was really touch-and-go, but something pushed me here."

"Really?" I said, under my breath. I wanted to care, but we weren't the same, he and I. I was basically flawless, while I could tell that he was riddled with them. And I'm not even talking about the dungarees. No — that ragged edge — he was probably grappling with a traumatic past involving bullying, neglect, and chocolate-biscuit addiction. Of course he'd had a hard time with his mind, but my mind was candyfloss all the way down.

"Want some advice?" he asked, still failing to read our small part of the busy room.

"Uh-huh," I said, just about.

He let off a grin like a firework. "Don't quit. Whatever you do, don't quit."

Why would I need to quit? I wondered, until he went quiet long enough for me to be able to read the daily timetable.

4:00am - Morning wake-up bell
4:30–6:30am - Meditate in the hall or in your room
6:30–8:00am - Breakfast break
8:00–9:00am - Group meditation in the hall
9:00–11:00am - Meditate in the hall or in your room according to the course leader's instructions
11:00–12:30 - Lunch break and rest
12:30–2:15pm - Meditate in the hall or in your room
2:30–3:30pm - Group meditation in the hall

3:45–5:15pm - Meditate in the hall or in your room according to the course leader's instructions
5:15–6:00pm - Tea break
6:00–7:00pm - Group meditation in the hall
7:00–8:15pm - Course leader's discourse in the hall
8:15–9:00pm - Group meditation in the hall
9:30pm - Retire to your room—lights out

There was an awful lot of meditation and terribly little anything else.

"The really good stuff doesn't happen until day five or six," the man-bear said.

"Cool," I said, but what I was actually thinking was *WHO THE HELL WOULD DO THIS FIVE TIMES?*

"Does it get easier each time?" I asked, when my curiosity got the better of me.

He considered it, stroking his long, tatty, LARPer's beard. "It gets... *different* hard."

"Why do you keep doing it, then?"

He inhaled deeply, as if the intoxicating scent of self-knowledge had just wafted in. "You'll see."

"Terrific." I turned to the last page of the pamphlet, where they'd hidden all the rules.

Meditators agree to:
1. Abstain from killing any being
2. Abstain from stealing
3. Abstain from all sexual activity
4. Abstain from telling lies
5. Abstain from all intoxicants

Returning meditators agree to also:
1. Abstain from eating after midday
2. Abstain from sensual entertainment and bodily decoration

3. *Abstain from using high or luxurious beds*

No wonder this ginger wizard was so apprehensive, nervously babbling trite advice at strangers. Ten days without dinner would terrify me. I skipped a meal once, back in 1999, but I was unconscious at the time, and I ate two dinners the following day to make up for it. And what the hell was sensual entertainment, anyway? Yoga? Porn? Belly dances?

I was called to a table. Behind it sat a row of three volunteers. Everyone working at the centre was a volunteer, I'd just read. They all had one thing in common — wide, baboonish grins, as if they'd just heard the world's greatest joke but couldn't possibly repeat it. It was need-to-know, you see.

"Did you read the pamphlet?" one of the volunteers asked. He looked like a young Uri Geller: thin nose, angular jaw, and intense, narrow eyes.

"I did, yes."

"Good. Phone?"

I reached into my trouser pocket, feeling for its outline. For ten days, she wouldn't be able to reach me, should she need me. Not that I had been much use lately, or perhaps ever. And it wasn't going to work, anyway. She'd been clear about that. I felt the same. I'd just never admitted that to her. I pulled out the phone and handed it over.

"You don't have another phone on you somewhere, do you?" the guy asked.

"No."

"No phone?" he pressed, his smile slipping only briefly before he noticed and caught it. "Not anywhere?"

"Do people really hide a second phone on themselves?"

"You'd be surprised," he said, pushing over a piece of paper with the rules. "Sign here."

I picked up the pen but noticed my hand was reluctant to sign. Why? What did I have to lose other than chicken, masturbation, and time? Certainly nothing important like my mind, right?

I forced my hand down to the line and scribbled my name.

4

After check-in, cushions wedged into my armpit, bag over my shoulder, I heaved myself along the narrow pathway into the first accommodation block, searching for room five. There were no locks on any of the doors, I noticed, before remembering we had nothing worth stealing.

Room five was on the left of the corridor, just past the squeaky-clean shared bathrooms. There was a smell of pine in the air and the heat was thick with pollen. Silently praying I wouldn't have a roommate, since they hadn't banned snoring, I pushed down on the handle.

Inside, I found a narrow room with two single pine beds in a line along the left wall. A tall piece of rectangular wood between them offered at least the hint of privacy, if we were both in our beds, tight to the wall. Did we really need that? We wouldn't be in here much anyway and when we were, we'd probably just be sleeping. Bedding lay folded at the foot of each bed. *Damn*.

The muted room tried so hard not to make a statement that it actually shouted its sadness. There were no framed pictures of sunsets; no flamboyant swashes of colour; no inspirational quotes from the Buddha or the Dalai Lama.

The rural location, many rules, and austere decoration made me feel as if I'd arrived for the first day at military school.

The bees were quieter now; being away from Evelyn had calmed them. I unzipped my sports holdall, all the time expecting a barrel-chested, be-hatted man to storm in and insult me in limerick. Inside the bag, she'd packed underwear, some T-shirts, my water bottle, toiletries, three new pairs of thick jogging bottoms — perhaps to protect my knees while I meditated? Were you allowed to meditate on your knees?

I wasn't sure. I'd never really done any. I'd copy the others.

The door opened, and I turned and began to salute before stopping myself, pretending to rub my head. My roommate was a short, clean-shaven man wearing sunglasses. He had neat brown hair of no distinguishable style, cream chinos, shiny black leather shoes, and a blue Ralph Loren polo top; neat but generic.

"Ah, good," he said, in German.

"Hallo," I replied, and held out my hand. He took it firmly and tried to shake it clean off. His smile didn't reach his eyes, which were skittish. Noble Silence didn't begin until the following morning, so we could talk.

"I'm Freddie," he said, continuing in German. "You don't meet a lot of Freddies in Germany, I know. My name is the only unusual thing about me."

I had met a lot of Freddies in Germany, but I didn't want to deny him the one thing he seemed to think he had going for himself.

"You don't look like the others either," he said.

I looked down at myself — blue jeans lightly splattered with chocolate, a plain blue T-shirt, scuffed brown leather shoes. As ensembles went, I felt the only firm statement my

20

outfit made was one of general indifference. The room and I had a lot in common.

"How do they look?" I asked, wondering if he'd also met the ginger bear. He flashed a toothy smile. Straight, those teeth.

"Oh, you know the type." He put his hand on the wall, easy to do in a room this narrow. "Counter-culture, aren't they? Hippies and the like. Man buns. Vegans. Jugglers." He said *jugglers* with a tone usually reserved for paedophiles.

I nodded, because I had noticed a certain grubby, mother earthiness to the group, had a vague feeling they were probably at home with homeopathy. Evelyn called these kinds of people crunchy. There was more crunch here than a paddling pool of popcorn.

"Yeah, I'm just your typical small-town kind of guy," Freddie said, bouncing on the spot. "A villager, really, you know? No nonsense. Swim with the stream. In the pack and fine with that."

I was used to Germans immediately switching to English when they heard my accent, but Freddie stuck to German, a sign he was outside my usual demographic. He had a light Bavarian accent but I could follow him, just about, and even if I didn't catch every word, there were so many words that my ears were always full.

"I don't think your typical villager does a Vipassana retreat," I said.

He puffed out his chest. "Well, something needs to change, doesn't it?" He lowered his chin. I sensed he was deciding whether he wanted to tell me his capital *T* Truth. "My wife just up and left me. This is going to be my third divorce." He raised three fingers. "Crazy, right? Each time you plan a wedding you think it will be your last. Of all that hoo-ha. All those people watching." His mouth narrowed. "They were my fault. All three."

Panic poked me in both eyes. Having blocked the door with his compact frame, he was now unburdening himself all over me. I didn't know what to do or say. "I'm sure they weren't just your fault?" I tried, while thinking about my three serious girlfriends before Evelyn. Had those breakups been my fault? Two had been, I suppose. The other was a result of her leaving me for someone else, sort of. It was weird, but I didn't think about it much. It didn't help to.

I realised something — although I'd loved those women, I'd also never once considered making a human with them. Never believed, not even on our best mornings, when our skies were clearest and hearts fullest, that our particular blend of genes and personalities and circumstances would create a worthy addition to this world.

Then I'd met Evelyn and known almost instantly that it would.

Freddie rubbed at his hair, which didn't seem to notice. "Something needs to change," he said again. "*I* have to change, I suppose. If you're always at the scene of the crime, bloody knife in your hand, at some point you need to accept you're the murderer, right?"

"I suppose so, Freddie, yeah." I shrugged and tried to turn back to the bed, back to my bag. "Anyway, these socks aren't going to —"

"Have you meditated much before?" he asked.

"Bits and bobs," I said, which was an exaggeration.

"Not really my scene either. Surprised it's anyone's scene, really." He frowned. "But needs must. And I need."

"I had some app thing," I said. "Didn't really stick."

"I hear that." He crossed his arms. "I had one too. No, I had three or four, even. Used them for like a week. Not much sticks to me. Not even wives."

I let out a small squeak of pity. We stood there, nodding a little at each other, while I angled my body away slowly, back towards my socks, wondering why everyone here was so open and confessional. It's a rare trait, to be able to admit when you get things wrong. An excellent trait. Not that I was wrong about anything.

"It was the neighbour," he said. "She left me for the neighbour. Can you believe that, Adam? My next-door fucking neighbour."

Squeezed in with so much of Freddie's failure, I began to feel claustrophobic in the small room. "Oh no," I said, and turned around to open the window.

"I see them sitting in his garden," he continued, wearily, digging his nails into his forearm. "Each morning at breakfast. They laugh a lot. He eats eggs. Poached. She eats the same muesli she always ate when we..." He faded out.

"Everyone laughs a lot in the beginning, Freddie. The beginning is easy."

"I've put the house up for sale now." He swallowed. "Quit my job too."

"Wow. That's... a lot?"

He drove his fist into his palm. "I'm going all in, buddy. This has to work, whatever it is. Meditation and all that hoo-ha. I'll make it work." He finally took off his sunglasses, slipping one stem into the collar of his polo top. "Only problem is, well, I kind of like to talk, you know? To spin a yarn. I mean, I really like to talk. My mum used to say what a shame it was that I got a mouth so keen on talking but a brain not interested in thinking."

I bit my tongue. What kind of mother says things like that?

"Used to get in trouble for that in the factory," he continued. "Chatting. In the end, they put me with a deaf guy." He winked. "Didn't shut me up."

23

"What do... I mean *did* you do for work?"

"Assembled furniture." He sighed. "Yeah. Fifteen years spent building crap on a production line. Wardrobes. Sideboards. Filing cabinets." He mimicked ironing. "Even ironing boards, one year. Bleak that was. Ironing, what a sham, you know? Tables though, mostly. They'd come in, come past you, you turn some screws, they disappear. You never see them again. FIFTEEN YEARS OF THAT."

I nodded as if I understood. I'd worked on a production line when I was sixteen. For a long two months.

"I'm planning a world trip," he said, brightening. "Once this is over."

I smiled. "That's great, Freddie. Really great."

"Yeah, I can't just work to pay rent anymore. You get sick." He tapped his heart. "Sick in here. In the old ticker. What's the point of it? Just work, pay rent, work some more, pay more rent. Why? So your wife can leave you for the fucking neighbour again? It's pointless, is what it is."

I froze mid-blink. "What do you mean *again*?"

"Wife number two left for a neighbour as well."

"Same neighbour?"

"Two streets over, actually. I don't see them unless I walk the dog that way. I don't walk the dog that way. Dog keeps running next door looking for wife number three. I'll probably have to get rid of the dog. You want a dog?"

"No, thanks. Ever thought about moving to the city?" I asked. "It's less claustrophobic."

"Too many neighbours."

"Yeah, but no one expects you to know them."

"It's not me I'm worried about. I'm thinking about becoming a travel blogger," he said. "You think that's a good idea, maybe?"

I began a laugh that swerved into a cough. If you'd let me guess potential careers for Freddie-the-typical-villager, at a rate of one guess per second, I'm confident I wouldn't have hit travel blogger before the end of the ten-day retreat. I didn't want to trample on his dream, but it was so lushly, crisply naïve that it simply begged to be flattened by the enormous feet of my pessimism. Being a travel blogger wasn't a job. It was barely even a hobby, and I could say that because I was sort of a travel blogger. But I only posted once a year, and all the text was bunched up and given an ISBN.

"You have any experience writing?" I asked.

"Nope. But I can learn."

"Travelling?"

"Never left Germany," he said, and thumped his heart. "But I have *belief*."

He said the word as if it were a magic spell against cynicism, and I suppose it was. That didn't mean it worked against reality, though.

"Why are *you* here?" he asked, rubbing his hands together.

"Me?" My eyes looped. "Oh... well... because my girlfriend forced me to come. Although I can understand why, just about. I sort of had to say yes."

"Yeses are tricky," he said. "Nos? Nos are a walk in a park." He shook his head. "You say no a thousand times then say yes once and boom, you're stuck. Committed."

"Are you talking about marriage, Freddie?" I asked, smiling at a memory suddenly playing in my mind's eye — a conversation with Evelyn in a park. That was why I was here, in a circuitous way. It was because of a yes. And a fig pie.

"Just saying," he said, bouncing his eyebrows. "Hey, maybe she wanted ten days on her own?"

"What? No."

"Do you know your neighbours?"

"Italian-German couple. They're nice."

"Handsome, the Italian?"

"She's not having an affair with the Italian, Freddie. Plus, that's the woman."

"Women," he said, as if about a stubborn weed. "They surprise you."

Evelyn surprised me often. In fact, her surprising nature was why I was in this room with Freddie, being further surprised by how quickly he was giving me close-up tours of his traumas. "It's you who makes your circumstances," he said.

"That so?" I asked, wondering why he'd made his circumstance living next door to his ex-wife and her new lover.

He lifted his chin. "One hundred percent."

I was souring on Freddie.

"No, 110 percent, actually," he said.

I flinched. Trying to make it seem like a shiver, I turned to close the window. Should Freddie be giving advice? What with him being a three-time divorced, non-writing travel blogger who'd never left Germany? Man-bear was no different. He was messed up enough to need five Vipassana retreats. There's an inverse correlation between how much people give advice and whether that advice should be listened to.

Freddie was a maze of contradictions. It was going to take him more than ten (silent) days to find his way out. I got the sense many people were here to make drastic changes to themselves and their lives. I just didn't understand why they thought sitting in silence would allow them to do so. Silence isn't clarity. It's just the absence of sound. And meditation wasn't about thinking, as far as I knew. It was about not thinking. When had that ever helped?

I turned back to my bed and continued unpacking. Forty-eight hours tops, I decided, for Freddie.

After a few hours talking to the other attendees and a bland rice and vegetable dinner, we retired to our room and, at nine thirty, switched the lights off.

"You can do this," Freddie said, into the darkness.

"I know."

"You have to."

"I don—" I stopped.

"*We* have to."

"Fine."

"Night then."

"Night."

"We can't talk anymore," he said. "Don't forget."

"Great."

"Not another word. Zip it, Freddie. This is it. Your big moment. Our big moment. We got this."

I said nothing.

"Don't let me talk again, okay?"

...

"Because I'll probably forget. I like to talk, you know? It's good talking. It helps."

...

"Right, well, good luck and everything. It's going to be a wild ride."

...

"Remember, you just have to believe in yourself."

...

"One hundred and ten percent."

5

Berlin, Germany, approximately two years before the retreat

"I made a pie," Evelyn said, as I tipped my head back and blinked into the sun shining through gaps in the leaves of the linden tree under which we were picnicking.

"Incredible," I said, as she fussed with Tupperware on the other side of the blanket. I watched, wondering how I had made this woman — twenty IQ points above me, three times my income, ten times my common sense — *my* woman?

Around us, dogs chased Frisbees, children chased dogs chasing Frisbees, and parents chased children chasing dogs chasing Frisbees.

"We were a great double act last night," she said, about a dinner party with our new neighbours, Max and Adriana, which we'd thrown to celebrate finally finishing redecorating the apartment — our first shared apartment. We'd poured two homes into one, and after a lick of paint, it was spectacular how well they'd merged. Any idiot could see that despite having nothing in common — in colour, pattern, or culture — her striped Turkish rug completed my ornate red-and-gold Iranian rug.

The Big Lebowski was wrong. It takes two rugs to tie a room together.

"We're very fun," I said. "The funnest people even, maybe?"

"For sure," she said, slicing into a pie with a blunt knife. Nearby, a man juggled. Another, shirtless and in tiny Speedos, strutted back and forth, showing off his enormous... calves. We'd spent the early morning cuddling in bed, the later morning cuddling on my scooter as we weaved through the city in search of brunch, and the last hour cuddling on this blanket.

She fed me pie from her hand.

"MMMMMMM," I moaned. "Fig, right? It's incredible that a woman who looks like you and thinks like you also cooks like you."

"See." She nodded. "I told you moving in together was a good idea."

"My waistline might not agree." I licked my lips. "More," I said, referring to the pie and to her and to the abundance of our shared lives. To this, the end of a long summer spent outdoors fusing our two friend groups.

"Oooh," she said, holding up her hand, palm open. "I found a little worm. Hello there, fella." She presented it to me as if it were a diamond, not a little fat brown wriggly tube.

"Yuck," I said, flinching.

"It's just a worm."

I turned away. "I don't like worms."

She dangled it over my head.

"Get away," I said, pushing her arm, but too aggressively, which only egged her on.

She tried to climb on top of me. "What's your problem with worms?"

"I don't have a problem with worms."

"Is your leg shaking?"

"No," I said, defensively. "Why would my leg be shaking?"

"You're afraid of worms." She laughed. "My god. What a wimp. It's just a cute little worm."

"They're not cute." I jutted out my chin. "And I'm not afraid of them."

"I'll put the worm back on the grass, okay?"

The jam session of nearby Turkish musicians erupted into knee slapping as the song they'd spent ten minutes patiently building rushed towards its frenetic conclusion. They cheered and then it went blissfully silent, before a baby burst into angry tears.

"Life's good, isn't it?" she said.

"You sound surprised?"

"Can you be nostalgic for something that hasn't ended?"

"No," I said. "I don't think so."

I dropped my head back on a cushion. She came and settled in next to me, head on my chest. I kissed the top of her head and my nostrils filled with her butter-coconut shampoo as my mind fizzed with scenes of zippy scooter rides through dense jungle to isolated huts stalked by cheeky troops of monkeys. "We have everything," I said.

She gave a small whimper. "I can think of one thing we don't have."

"A tiny dog that chases Frisbees?"

"Okay," she said. "Two things we don't have."

"Is the other thing a decorated third bedroom?" We hadn't got to that room. It lacked a purpose.

"A use for that bedroom."

"Do you think anyone has ever been as in love as we are

now?" I asked casually, as if requesting a napkin. She chuckled at the ridiculousness of the question, but when I didn't join the chuckle, she pulled away from me and sat up, embarrassment flushing her pale cheeks.

"I've never been this in love," she said, because she worked in politics and knew how to be diplomatic.

"I'll take it."

"You're very complimentary today," she said. "What's going on?"

"We're just young and in love and under a tree in my favourite park, eating fig pie."

"We're always in Hasenheide Park."

"I'm just..." I took a deep breath. "Feels like this is one of those moments, you know? Like when we're in a care home in our eighties, blankets over our laps, mindless TV droning on, I think it's days like today that our minds will drift to."

She nestled back down into my chest. "It's incredible, isn't it, that there was a time, only like a year ago, where I'd have been under this tree and you'd have been over there." She pointed in the vague direction of the tree line and a busy skate park. "And we'd have spent a whole Saturday like this near but not even looking at each other."

"Speak for yourself," I said with a laugh. "I'd have been secretly spying on you, drinking you in like the fine wine that you are while pretending to read my Kindle."

"That's sweet," she said. "And creepy." She patted my stomach. "They've been married four years. Max and Adriana. They're four years younger than us, yet already married for four years, which means they must have been together what, at least two years before that? That's six years. How long have we had together?"

"Not even a year."

"You're right," she said. "There's no rush. We have to enjoy this."

I had said nothing about a rush, but I felt as if there were one. That whatever this was — this particularly intoxicating, throwing-caution-to-the-wind, "yes" state — needed to be acted upon before it was overwhelmed by all the bad r's: rationality, reality, routine.

She sat up, folded her legs beneath her, and rooted around in her brown leather handbag for her phone. "I don't want to ruin this beautiful moment," she said. "But I have to go to my gynaecologist to pick up my pill prescription. They're closing at two. Can you take me on the scooter?"

"Let's have a child," I said, suddenly but nonchalantly.

Her brow furrowed. She went silent.

"Let's have a child," I repeated.

"Seriously?"

"It's time," I said. "We've tested us and we're doing very well. It's time," I said again, unnecessarily. "This love deserves to make a child. Did I really just say that? No." I slapped the picnic blanket and ground with my palm. "It's true. Let's do it. Let's multiply!"

The pie had gone straight to my head.

"We agreed to wait another six months then decide," she said.

"Fuck it."

She laughed. "That's it? 'Fuck it'?"

"Fuck it."

"It's hard to tell when you're serious."

"I'm rarely serious." I frowned because I assumed that's what serious people did. "I'm being serious. I think."

"Well," she said, pursing her lips and pulling back her head, viewing me from a reserved distance, as if I were explosive. "Wow."

"And if it works quickly, we'd have a summer baby, right?"

"Why does that matter?"

"It's better they're not born during term time."

"Why?"

"Then they won't get beaten up on their birthday."

"Why would you get beaten up on your birthday?"

"They don't do that here?" I asked.

"What? You've lost me."

"Never mind."

"I wish I shared your optimism for how easy it will be," she said, her voice quietening. The way she talked about her family's women, it was a miracle she'd ever become a branch on the withered family tree.

"How hard can it really be?" I gushed. "People make humans in the back row of cinemas. Don't get the prescription. Fuck it."

She took a long breath. "It's just... sudden?"

"How is it sudden? We've spent like a hundred hours discussing it."

"You're just..." Her nose twitched. "You can be kind of flippant. And what's that other F-word? For someone who changes their mind a lot?"

Evelyn was German, but you barely noticed. Her English was flawless and our relationship had begun in that language and I was sure would remain in it. She had too much of a head start for my German to catch up. "Fickle?"

"Sounds like a fruit for pies."

I laughed. "I won't change my mind. And it will work out. It basically always works out, right? Look how compatible we are, right down to our taste in music and choice of rugs and love of pies. Why would the universe swerve our lives together so spectacularly only to deny us the point of all this?" I said, waving my arms around, perhaps because there were so many babies around us. Almost all of them were crying.

"The universe doesn't care about us," she said. "That's not how the universe works. It's all just a big random soup."

"I refuse to believe it's a big random soup."

She smiled. "Okay. *Fine.* Let's fuck it."

"We're fucking it?" I dived towards her, knocking her over. I pinned her arms back and peppered her neck with deliberately sloppy kisses. "Really?"

"Ugh. Keep your tongue to yourself."

"We're really fucking it?" I said, letting her go.

Her grin was the answer. "I only have one condition."

"Shoot."

6

Day 1/10: AM
Location: Bed
Mood: Cautiously optimistic

At 4am, a gong sounded. I turned over and moaned.

Wait, is moaning allowed?

I sat up, regretting the moan, and vowed not to moan again.

But, I mean, really? Four in the morning?

Freddie put on the light and we dressed, avoiding eye contact, before sloping in single file down the corridor to the new two-storey meditation hall at the back of the complex.

It was time for our first meditation session. Two hours, which was one and a half hours more than all the meditation I'd ever done in my life. Total.

As I'd mentioned to Freddie, I'd half-heartedly begun a meditation practice three or four times but always stopped a few days in, never quite able to work out what I was supposed to feel, or learn, or get from it.

If this experience — ten days, twelve hours a day, in a setting of complete silence and focus — didn't reveal the answer to me, nothing would.

We stood outside, a bedraggled, crunchy mass of the recently sleeping, staring at the closed double doors, willing them to open so we could get busy with the humble work of self-betterment. Freddie had his hands deep in his tracksuit's pockets, believing in himself.

Another gong.

YoungUriGellar opened the doors.

Inside, on the first floor, we filed into the hall where one hundred and twenty meditation mats waited, sixty for the men, sixty for the women. The latter entered from the other end of the hall. It was a beautiful space with exposed wooden beams and enormous windows. No clocks. My spot was in the middle, second row from the back; I'd placed my things there the previous evening.

I fluffed my large red floor mat and then carefully shifted the smaller circular red meditation cushion until it was exactly in the centre. Satisfied with its plumpness and position, I dropped onto it. Most of my neighbours were already in the lotus position, eyes squeezed shut.

In front of us, at the back left and right of the hall, two doors opened simultaneously. From the left one came a small, inoffensive looking mouse of a man. He had silver circular glasses and, I suppose, also a nose and eyes and maybe even a chin, although barely. He took his place on a raised platform facing the male half of the hall, where an instructor would be if this were an exercise class.

This was our course leader.

The female course leader shuffled towards her raised bed. She was, conservatively, 214 years old. Her tufts of white hair that jutted out at wild angles of dishevelment. It appeared as though death had come for her several decades ago, discovered her meditating, assumed she was already dead, and never returned. She sat, stooping sharply to the left, like a collapsing shack ravaged by a storm.

I liked her.

She had something.

Or she'd had something.

The leaders closed their eyes, so I closed mine. This was it, I supposed. Probably. A man's voice warbled over unseen speakers and in a language I couldn't place. It was singing, the voice, sort of, but in a deep, croaky falsetto that sounded like a frog being smashed to death by a piece of plywood.

The warbling lasted ten hundred thousand million years.

I would later learn that the warbling was in Pali, the ancient language of both India and the Buddha. The man doing the warbling was Satya Narayan Goenka, an Indian-Burmese businessman turned meditation teacher who had died in 2013. His job — through the recordings that began and ended each session here, as well as through nightly video lectures — was to teach us the Vipassana technique. All 160 Dhamma Dharā centres around the world used his words and recordings.

"Obserrrve the breeeeath entering and leaving the nostrils," he said.

Long breath.

Soft moan.

He had an extremely unusual speaking style in that he sped up and slowed down randomly. He sounded like a bad community theatre actor doing an impression of a bad community theatre actor pretending to be Yoda having a seizure.

"Perhaps it enters the righttttttt nostril. Perhaps, sometimes, it even enters bbbbooooth nostrils simultaneously. SIMULTANEOUSLeeeeeY.

"Perhaps it enters the left nostril."

Dramatic pause.

Nasal breath.

Minor gurgle.

"Just OBserve it. Don't attempt to chaaaaaange the breath in any way. Just OBserve. Paaaaaatiently and persis-TANTleeey. Patiently and persisTANTleeey. Ardentleeeey. With a clear, equanimous mind."

Major gurgle.

Flamboyant wheeze.

It was a bumpy start between the two of us, but I put that down to the early hour and his off-key singing. I was happy he was here and could finally explain what I was supposed to feel, or learn, or get from meditation.

Only he didn't.

He just stopped.

The room fell silent.

I waited for more instructions.

Instead, an empty minute passed. I realised there were no more instructions coming. We were all alone, together, with ourselves.

It was 4:30am, for some stupid reason.

So, with a clear and equanimous mind, patiently and persistently, I attempted to observe the breath as it entered the left nostril, the right nostril, and sometimes even both nostrils simultaneously.

In... left nostril.

Out... right nostril.

In... left nostril.

Out... both nostrils.

Time passed. Thoughts came and went. Focus was found, then lost. I squirmed often. My thoughts wandered.

Some more time passed. I returned to the breath. Some more time passed, just about, maybe, I supposed?

In... both nostrils.

Out... both nostrils.

In... left nostril.

Out... left nostril.

They wandered off again, the thoughts. *That's okay*, I decided. The session was nearly over now, anyway. I opened my eyes and listened intently for the gong. What sweet relief it would be, that gong. My right knee was furious with me. In the break I could walk around, have some water, stretch, put the knee to use.

No gong though?

I closed my eyes and steeled myself, determined to do the best meditating possible — perhaps even the cleanest, crispest, most wholesome meditation the world had ever seen — for the few minutes that remained. I thought about cheddar cheese. Then Kate Bush. After that, a holiday with my parents to Disneyworld when I fell into a swimming pool in all my clothes and was so shocked I peed myself. Then a Spanish restaurant, reliving a particularly brutal semi-public breakup. Then Evelyn was fucking someone in our bed and I didn't enjoy watching it at all.

Had they forgotten the gong?

Where was the gong?

I could hit the gong.

I wandered out to the upstairs vestibule to check if perhaps the clock had stopped. We were free to come and go as we wanted, left to police ourselves. It said twenty-one minutes had passed. Looking at it, head askance, I felt as if something heavy had fallen on me. An anvil, for example. I hobbled back to my mat, got into a kneeling position, and tried to bury my rapidly growing fear under careful observation of my breath.

By the time Goenka's voice finally returned, at the end of the session, not to offer more instruction but just to warble another throaty song in Pali, both my legs were stumps and I was begging for relief.

"Take rest," he said, eventually, when I'd given up all hope.

This was one session?!

I looked around as people filed out of the room. How messed up did their lives have to be, that they were willing to subject themselves to this?

When I could walk, I wandered outside too, keeping my Noble Silence. I stretched for five minutes. The fear that had been nibbling at me since I got out of bed that morning was now taking great toothy chunks from my self-belief.

I can't do this.

I won't make it.

I have to quit.

But then what about her? What about us?

And then I'll be a quitter. Could I handle that?

I walked around in a confused daze.

Another gong.

Another session.

Blissfully, Goenka's singing lasted only a few miserable, off-key minutes this time.

"Obserrrve the breeeeath entering and leaving the nostril. Perhaps it enters the left nostril. Perhaps it enters the right nostril. Perhaps sometimes it even enters bbbbooooth nostrils simultaneously. SIMULTANE-OUSLeeeeeY. You are not here to control or regulate the breath. If it is deep, it is deep. If it is shallow, it is shallow. If it is passing through the left nostril, you are aware. If it is passing through the right nostril, you are aware. If it is passing through both nostrils simultaneously, you are aware. Just observe reality as it is, not as you would like it to be."

Stalker-on-the-telephone breathing.
Elegant whimper.

"Paaaaaaaatiently. Ardently but persistently. Consistently. Diligently."

Ribbit ribbit.
Nasal fart.

"You are booooooound to be successful. Bound to be successfULLL."

He was a fan of repetition, I was learning.

We meditated again, left alone with our minds. I found that no matter how much I tried to keep mine on a leash, it kept escaping and running off in pursuit of fun. Four breaths, five breaths, not more. I stayed, regardless. Sat there. Concentrated. Followed Goenka's instructions while having a deeply miserable time.

In... right nostril.

Out... right nostril.

In... left nostril.

Out... both nostrils.

This second session was both mental and physical torture. I had obviously made a terrible mistake. And it was her fault. Why had she sent me here?

I opened my eyes and looked around. Everyone else appeared to be with the program, meditating dutifully. If the other hundred and nineteen people in the room could do this, why couldn't I? What did they have that I didn't?

Many things, I would soon find out.

7

Somehow, feeling like a vicious, club-wielding mob had attacked me, I made it through that first day of meditation.

More than the pain, confusion, and sadness, what had got to me was just the raw, jagged shock of it — of being so wrong and unprepared. No matter what I'd told Evelyn — and long believed about myself — this process had already revealed that I didn't have control of my mind.

In a couple of the sessions, I'd chased away my raging thoughts, thinking of little more than the breath as it washed in and out, but for a maximum of ten consecutive breaths.

In others, I'd been lucky to make it three or four breaths before my mind, whirling non-stop like some kind of out-of-control horror-house ride, raced me through thoughts, memories, words, songs, ideas, hopes, and fears.

In... left nostril.

Out... right nostril.

In... both nostrils.

And this was just day one. My body was doing what bodies always did in times of shock and hardship: screaming at me to run away. My mind agreed vehemently. The two were a formidable team and took turns clobbering my resolve with those clubs.

Everything hurt.

I stayed, of course, but really only because I was too embarrassed to quit on day one. To admit that I was the weakest amongst one hundred and twenty people? How would I live that down?

As we waited in the meditation hall's downstairs vestibule for our first nightly Goenka video lecture, Freddie looked just as shell-shocked as I felt. Our eyes met briefly, his scared and distant. I tried to remember when I'd last been this miserable. Not since my school days. Not that I thought about my school days.

Another gong. The door to the lecture hall opened. Each evening, we'd watch a recorded "Dhamma Discourse" video lecture so Goenka could explain what we'd learned that day and what was coming during the next.

I was certainly full of questions, the most urgent being why focusing mechanically, repeatedly, endlessly on the breath entering and leaving my nostrils was worth my time. The next being why I was failing so spectacularly at what seemed the simplest task imaginable.

We trooped into the room. We weren't allowed to lie down, but I snagged a spot against the wall, where I could at least rest my weary back. Our bespectacled course leader, who reminded me of a high school counsellor bullied by his seniors, started the projector. When Goenka appeared, the course leader smiled at him as if reunited with a long-lost friend. Perhaps he was. The video was part of a lecture series recorded in 1991. Goenka sat, lotus-ed, next to his wife, who said nothing and looked confused about why she was there.

Goenka talked; Goenka loved to talk. He and Freddie had that in common. My heart sank when he began with a warning that these nightly talks weren't for any kind of intellectual entertainment. They were to help us understand the technique.

"The first day is full of great difficulties and discomforts, partly because one is not accustomed to sitting all day long and trying to meditate, but mostly because of the type of meditation that you have started practicing: awareness of respiration — nothing but respiration."

He explained that the mind always runs to either the past or the future to escape an unhappy present. And yet, Goenka argued, the present is where we live. The past is gone, and the future doesn't exist, so it's only understanding, no, *accepting* the present reality that matters. Our breath is real and only ever in the present, so we focus on the breath.

Simple, no? Which isn't the same as easy, of course.

"Tomorrow will be a little easier, next day more so. Little by little, all the problems will pass away, if you work. Nobody else can do the job for you; you have to do the work yourself. You have to explore reality within yourself. You have to liberate yourself."

Then he ran through his greatest hits:

"Patiently and persistently. Ardently. With a clear and equanimous mind, you are bound to be successful."

Then he sang again, of course. If I'd had anything to throw, I'd have thrown it at the screen. Instead, I put my fingers in my ears until he stopped, and then I stood and huffed my way back upstairs, trying to convince myself that he was building slowly, couldn't let all his rabbits out of his hat on day one, and then as another gong sounded, I began the last, miserable, monotonous, arduous meditation session.

An interminable, incommunicable amount of stretched and warped time later, he finally said the magic words: "Take rest."

It was over; I was free. I could move. I could lie down. I could indulge my ego and forget about my breath, could take it for granted, as usual. I could sleep. First, I walked around for forty minutes, a small gift of apology to my body, then crashed into bed.

Another gong; lights out.

One day down, nine to go.

NINE TO GO?

What the hell is this?

Why am I doing it?

Why is anyone else?

At 4am, the gong rang out again. Freddie got up and put on his shoes. I tried to open my eyes, but someone had glued them shut.

8

Day 2/10: AM
Location: Bed
Mood: Deeply sombre

Twisting and turning, I tried to convince myself to get up. That it was just two teeny tiny hours of meditation. What were they, really, in the grand scheme of things? And what's the point in meditating if you're so tired you keep falling asleep? It takes work to leash your mind and work needs energy, which you get from sleep, obviously.

Probably.

And ten hours of meditation was plenty. Too much, even, I felt sure. If I skipped the sessions, I could rise at the civilised hour of 6:30am — rested and perhaps even able to saunter out for breakfast. After that meal, my belly full, I could then stroll through the woods and meadow as a small gesture of apology for all the horrible things I would do to my body that day.

I was sure Evelyn would understand. And so, when the next gong rang, Freddie — who, let's face it, was a basket case and needed this much more than I did — slipped out of the room while I, decision made, rolled towards the wall and drifted back to sleep confident my rationale was unassailable.

Six thirty arrived as everything did here: by express gong delivery. I didn't saunter, too scared of the day ahead, but I did walk briskly to the canteen, the same large room in which we'd first checked in. I joined the back of the queue, feeling guilty I'd spent the last hours slumbering while they'd all been "observing the natural breath to concentrate the mind."

At the front of the queue was a counter. In the middle of that, a huge urn of porridge. The queue split in two, half moving down the front of the counter, half down the back. After ladling our porridge, we were supposed to stop at the wicker baskets of fruit, which we'd slice on little wooden cutting boards. Artificial sugar was banned, so I knew those fruits were the best chance I had of sweetening the food, and perhaps with it, my demeanour.

I was salivating by the time I reached the urn, my tongue hanging out of my mouth as though I were a dog begging at the back of a butcher. I scooped two generous spoons of thick porridge into my plastic orange bowl, trying to ladle quickly, knowing how many sets of hungry postmorning-meditation eyes were watching me, willing me along the counter, just as I'd been watching and willing moments before, judging people who took too much, or dawdled.

I moved to the baskets of fruit and began slicing up an overripe pear and then an apple. Opposite me, on the other side of the counter, cutting his fruit, was a tall, athletic man with narrow brown eyes, a prominent jaw, and a single thick ponytail of blond hair that reached his shoulder blades. He worked quickly and methodically. I knew nothing about this man's life, yet I felt sure that he:

Had ridden a horse, bareback.

Wrote poetry to the smell of incense.

Had felled a tree, shirtless.

Sitting between us was a bowl for the fruit cores and any other waste. Finished with my apple, I dropped its core in. I was about to put down my knife and step away from the counter when the man stopped cutting his own apple, reached forward, and picked *my* discarded apple core out of the waste bowl.

I froze, as did time, but then again, time was perpetually frozen here. He put my apple core on his cutting board and cut some insignificant, infinitesimally small pieces from its flesh.

A hot shower of shame washed over me. I mean, the effrontery. He was publicly chastising me for wastefulness, and in this holier-than-thou setting. They had seen, all of them, I was sure. Were now quietly condemning me in the snap, crackle, and pop of their crunchy minds.

Now, in this man's defence, I'm not a man of precision. I'm sloppy, slapdash, a perennial corner cutter, exception expecter, and edge-case enthusiast. Even so, his public pedantry was too much. And so, standing there, glowering at him, my left hand burning from the warmth of the porridge in the stupid plastic bowl, I looked as close to this man's eyes as I dared and scowled with immense vitriol.

It was the sharpest single scowl of my life. Sharper than the knife in my hand, which, I saw now, was tilted at just the angle necessary to flick out his eye if I lunged forward over the counter and believe me, this was what I wanted to do most in the universe. What I probably would have done, were our universe repercussionless.

Sorry. I mean, I would have tried to remove his eye but would have cut so poorly that he would have had to follow up, going back into his own eye socket to cut the last scraps of optic nerve, perhaps while tutting or rolling his other eye.

His good eye.

Although I imagined he'd look good with one eye.

He'd probably get a parrot.

He probably already had a parrot.

I put down the knife, just about, eventually, and shuffled away while swearing that in this life or the next (he almost certainly believed in some form of reincarnation) I would get bloody revenge upon him and his family, and maybe also his pets.

Excessive, you're thinking?

A trifle over the top?

Hyper-hyperbolic for such a minor act?

Perhaps, but in this setting, minor acts were enormous. NOTHING HAPPENED HERE. There was no gossip, scandal, news, or entertainment (sensual or otherwise). There were no interactions of any kind. All you could do was watch people as they moved around doing trivial, mundane things. We had interacted, AppleFuckFace and I. Before the end of this day, everyone would have a nickname, because why not?

I had the time.

Oh lordy, did I have the time.

Time was all I had.

And shame. I was wet through with shame.

I ate my porridge in silence, as did everyone else, yet I knew my silence was heavier than theirs. Occasionally I looked over at AppleFuckFace, hoping he might choke on a small piece of my ill-gotten apple. Instead, he sat there smiling beatifically with his youthful, jouster's vitality.

Being sure not to waste even a tiny drip of my not-sweet-enough porridge, I washed up and stomped outside and around and around and around the woods trying to work out how I'd ended up in this situation, with so much meditation ahead of me and yet nothing to learn about myself.

And then... I was hit with a force of insight so sudden and violent that I tripped over a tree root and stumbled forward and bit a little corner of my tongue. It was something Goenka had said in the Dhamma Discourse the previous evening: this retreat was a deep, surgical cut into our subconscious, and it would release a lot of pus.

My subconscious. What if I handled it just as sloppily and inattentively as I did the apples I sliced? Would that not mean all the posturing I'd done about how I was completely mined and knew myself really well and had met all my traumas and demons head-on was... a lie?

That might mean there was a lot of pus still down there. A lot of meat I had not cut from the flesh of my past indiscretions. That thought terrified me, and just as I was thinking of hopping the small fence between that craphole of a town and me, some idiot rang a gong, and I had to go meditate.

9

The first five minutes of every meditation session of day one and two

OH GOD PLEASE GOD NO GOD I'LL DO ANYTHING.

I'd fall onto my cushion, sighing, rubbing my thighs and feet and the lumps in my back.

I'd tell myself I was an idiot a few times while counting how many sessions I'd completed that day and how many more lay ahead and then how many more days remained. Not believing the figure could still be so high, I'd count them again.

The figure would still be as high.

OH GOD PLEASE GOD NO GOD I'LL DO ANYTHING.

I'd fantasise about how it might feel to leave this place on day eleven. I'd fantasise about leaving this place immediately, about hiding in a plush hotel with extra fluffy dressing gowns until day eleven, then going home pretending I'd breezed through the retreat and learned crucial things about myself that I'd keep stubbornly vague.

Lotus position again?
Kneel?
Sit with my legs up?
What did it matter? They were all equally shit.
Lotus then, since everyone else seemed to favour it.
I'd fold my legs and try to ignore the shooting pain flaring in my hips. I'd wiggle deeper into my cushion, trying to awaken the parts of me already numb from the previous sessions.

OH GOD PLEASE GOD NO GOD I'LL DO ANYTHING.

Goenka would sing. My stomach would bubble with hot, acidic anger. I'd remember that while he was singing, I wasn't technically required to be meditating. Also, if he was singing — which is at least what he thought he was doing — time had to be passing (however slowly), which meant we were moving nearer the end of this block of meditation.

Yay.
Oh, he's stopped singing.
The session has started, Adam.
Right, yep, sorry, Adam.
I'd shut my eyes.
Okay, Adam, this is going to be a good one.
Yes, Adam, I know.
Focus on the breath then, lad. Let's go.

In... left nostril.
Out... left nostril.
In... right nostril.
Out... both nostrils.

Why am I doing this? This is stupid.

THINKING
Back to the breath.

In... both nostrils.
Out... both nostrils.
In... left nostril.
Out... right nostril.

You're a fraud.

THINKING
Back to the breath.

In... left nostril.
Out... left nostril.
In... left nostril.
Out... both nostrils.

Running the hill. Been running up that God. DIFFERENT FACES.

SINGING
Back to the breath.

In... both nostrils.

What's that noise? Oh, it's a man crying. What a strange cry he has. He sounds like a goat trapped in a bucket. At least you're not a goat trapped in a bucket. At least you're not crying like that, in front of everybody. Not yet. You lost your dog one time. Do you remember that? Did he get trapped in a bucket? No, it was in a wood. The woods had a flasher. Your mum was flashed by him once. She shouted "Is that all you've got!" and he ran away. Your mum is a nice lady. You should call your mum more. You're a piece-of-shit son.

THINKING
Back to the breath.

In... left nostril.
Out... both nostrils.

Come on baaaaaby. Come on darrrrling. YOU AND ME. I'D MAKE A DEAL. OOOOOOOOHHHHH. Been running up that God. DIFFERENT FACES.

SINGING
Back to the breath.

The only good page in this book is page seventy-two, and that's because it's blank. Remember that review of your second book? Brutal. BRUTAL. People can be so cruel. You're a piece-of-shit writer too.

THINKING
Back to the breath.

In... both nostrils.

The colour purple is nice. Someone should invent more colours. Some women have extra cones. Do I have all my cones? That documentary about cones mentioned that there was a certain type of fish that has, like, a million? They can see a thousand purples. But they're still a fish. What's the point of being a fish? What's the point of anything? What's the point in nihilism? Good point. Life is meaningless, but not worthless. That's good. Did I make that up or is it a quote? Probably I made it up. I'm very smart. Narrowly.

THINKING
Back to the breath.

In... left nostril.
Out... left nostril.
In... right nostril.
Out... right nostril.

Remember that time when you were six and your parents bullied you into taking part in a Picture of Health contest that you lost to a fat kid? Chocolate. Some chocolate would be great. Not for the fat kid, but for you. Where's that kid now, I wonder? I bet he went places. Slowly.

THINKING
Back to the breath.

In... left nostril.
Out... left nostril.
In... right nostril.
Out... right nostril.

Do you remember when you tried to learn the ukulele? What a farce. Do you remember when you tried to learn the guitar? What a farce. Do you remember when you tried to learn the piano? What a farce. Do you remember how many times you've come close to buying a violin? You are a farce. Goenka is more musical than you.

Farce — good band name? The Farces — better?
It must be nearly an hour now, right?

THINKING
Back to the breath.

ARGH. MY HIP. OUCH. STUPID HIP. STUPID VIPASSANA. STUPID MEDITATION. STUPID GOENKA. STUPID EVELYN.

COMPLAINING
Back to the breath.

In... both nostrils.
Out... right nostril.
In... both nostrils.
Out... both nostrils.
In... both nostrils.
Out... left nostril.

You did six breaths without thinking! You're getting better at this. Actually, you're doing great. You're a meditation god. You are so good at this. It's incredible how good you are at this. If only people knew how incredible you are at this. You should tell people. You should write a book. You could be the new Goenka.

It must be nearly an hour now, right?
Fuck, I'm thinking.
You are?
We are.
I'm not.
We're talking to each other.
Oh, yeah. Weird.

THINKING
Back to the breath.

In... both nostrils.
Out... right nostril.

Someone else is weeping. Poor bastard. Shouldn't someone help him? No, just ignore him. He has to do the work himself. Goenka says so.
Running down the hill. Running up that street. OOOOOOOHHHHHH. SWAP OUR FACES.
Book idea: The Fine Art of Incompetence — How to fail at everything with a stunning lack of grace.

THINKING
Back to the breath.

In... right nostril.
Out... left nostril.

Remember that guy at university, Piss Tom? How he turned away from you in an Irish bar, peed discreetly into his pint, then offered it to you? You said "Is that piss, Tom", and he said, nonchalantly, as if telling you the time, "Yeah, it is."

THINKING
Back to the breath.

In... both nostrils.
Out... both nostrils.
In... left nostril.

Were hazelnuts named by a Hazel? Aren't all nuts technically monkey nuts? There is so much to know about nuts. It's nuts. Oooh, I did a pun. Don't pun. You're a piece of shit. No, you're the greatest. You're the greatest piece of shit.

THINKING
Back to the breath.

In... left nostril.
Out... left nostril.

Business idea: Sibling Swap — a platform in which people who have nothing in common with their siblings can give them to only children looking for a second-hand brother or sister. Legally binding.

THINKING
Back to the breath.

Evelyn doesn't really love you. She's just pretending. No one loves you. You are not lovable. You know this. Everyone knows this. She's fucking other men right now in your bed. Real men. Taut men. Men with shoulders. Men with cars. Men with whisky collections. Men called Glenn with Glens.

THINKING
Back to the breath.

So, Adam, looking out at this adoring crowd of your many fans, how do you feel about having finally won the Booker prize? I'm humbled. Even in my wildest dreams and fantasies and inner monologues, I never once imagined standing here before you, collecting this prestigious award. I know there was a geography teacher at your high school who said you'd probably end up working in McDonald's all your life. Anything you want to say to him? Are you Happy Meal now, McMotherfucker? Actually, no, don't tell him that. It's really lame. I've nothing to say. My achievements speak for themselves. What are they exactly? Didn't I win the Booker prize? Ha, yeah right. The only good page was blank.

THINKING
Back to the breath.

Do you remember that time at school with the worm?

THINKING
Back to the breath.

Do you remember that time at school where they put your head down the —

THINKING
Back to the breath.

Do you remember that time at sch —

THINKING
Back to the breath.

Why do you never think about school? School matters. It was years and years and years. I think you think you're better than your school. That you're better than your hometown. But you're not. You're a fraud. A fake. You're still that tiny, bullied child, and if you have a child, it will be a tiny, bullied child too.

THINKING
Back to the breath.

You don't love her either, you know. She's just very attractive. She's a trinket. You'll defriend her like you defriend everyone else because she's not fun anymore. If only you were as surgical at cutting fruit as you are at cutting people out of your life. You are a piece of shit.

THINKING
Back to the breath.

Two more rounds. That's it. You will have tried everything. You won't come back from that. Neither will she. Look at her. She's falling apart and you're hiding. You're hiding so much she sent you here, the one place where there's nowhere to hide. A place which will be your undoing. You are coming undone. This is just the start. You are a shit lover. And a shit friend. No, I'm not. They don't deserve me, any of them. I am fine. I am kind. Narrowly. I am flawed, but so are they. They are more flawed. I was fine before her and I will be fine after her. I am one of the greats.

THINKING
Back to the breath.

Come on baby. Feel how it feels. OOOOOHHHHH. YOU AND ME. I CAN. I COULD. I'D MAKE A DEAL.

SINGING
Back to the breath.

You should run away. You used to run away all the time. Running away is really underrated. Do you remember that month in Bangkok? That was glorious. Wake up, put a dot on a map, go there. Skytrain. Practically rained sriracha. Food from witches' cauldrons right out on the street. The air as thick as yoghurt. How it smelt after it rained? You were free then. What happened to you? You could go back there. You're still young. You're still desirable. Narrowly.

THINKING
Back to the breath.

In... right nostril.
Out... both nostrils.
In... left nostril.

Why did you never write about your trip to Iran? Why are you still writing travel memoirs? No one cares about your life. Oooh, I went on holiday and now the world should know?

THINKING
Back to the breath.

You are the greatest. Hang in there. Recognition is coming. No one else has what you have, kid. You are the special one. You have a gift. You are chronically unappreciated. No one as good as you can stay in the shadows forever.

THINKING
Back to the breath.

You suck. You are terrible. You are a hack. You are the sad dying fart of a sad dying sack of sad dying shit.

THINKING
Back to the breath.

I hate golf. Golf is the absolute goddamn worst.

In... right nostril.
Out... left nostril.

It has to be an hour now, right? Was that the gong? It wasn't the gong. Strange, because it's been so long. Yeah, it's definitely time. It's late. They're late. The session has to end. It has to end now. I can't do this. OH GOD PLEASE GOD NO GOD I'LL DO ANYTHING. *It hurts. Back. Ankle. Thigh. Knee.* OH GOD PLEASE GOD NO GOD I'LL DO ANYTHING. *I can't do this. I can't do this. I'm going crazy. Why am I doing this?* OH GOD PLEASE GOD NO GOD I'LL DO ANYTHING.

DESPAIRING
Back to the breath.

10

Berlin, Germany, approximately one and a half years before the retreat

I groaned and closed the tab; another school crossed off the list. I had only three left in my master Berlin Education Excel spreadsheet. A calendar notification popped up on the bottom right of the screen:

Two becomes one becomes three? Sexy sex sex (*the bed*)

Calendar spam now too? Those internet tricksters were getting more creative by the day. I clicked it away as Evelyn appeared at the door.

"Whatcha doing?" she said. "I can hear you groaning through the wall."

I swivelled towards her on my office chair and lifted my legs onto the bed, availing myself of the chair's generous tilt. "Every school around here is a clusterfuck. We need to move ASAP."

"Who says ASAP?"

"People who have just read the school reports I've read."

"What's up with that big school near the supermarket?"

"It's on special measures. I was just reading an interview with the headteacher, who said their biggest issue is violence and that they're planning to turn around"—I made air quotes—"'disadvantaged youths through sport-based interventions'."

"Yuck," she said, coming into the room and lying down on her side of the bed. "Sport."

"We have to move," I said, with commendable earnestness.

"We don't even have a child. We're not even close to having a child. It never works. We're screwing like crazy and it never works. Every month is the same sad rollercoaster of hope then despair."

"Despair?" I certainly wasn't despairing. "It's only been six months."

"Yeah," she said, quietly. "Six months."

"Well, the longer it takes, the more the schools will have gentrified, I suppose. There's always that. I'm not sending our child somewhere they'll be shanked for their lunch money."

She frowned. "Was your school really that bad? You never talk about it."

"I..." I hesitated. "There's no reason to."

"We're not moving," she said. "I can't worry what school it's going to *and* whether it will exist. One problem at a time."

She was focusing on the wrong problem. Yes, she wasn't pregnant yet, but it had only been six months.

I took a deep breath. "I want our child to go to school in a dilapidated farmhouse in a charming French village with just three other students and frequent pony rides."

"This apartment is nice and cheap and the area..." She took my pillow and put it on top of hers and turned onto her back. "It can't get any worse, can it?"

"A woman was shooting up in the entranceway today."

"Well," she said, chuckling, "the homeless guy who was living on the stairs hasn't been back in two days. So, there's that, right?"

I scratched the stubble on my cheek but said nothing, dreaming of pony rides.

"You see my calendar invite?" she asked, licking her lips.

My eyes rounded. "That was *you*?"

"Some things are going to change," she said.

"Six months isn't long."

"Seriously? It's been the longest six months of my life."

"Okay," I said, wondering why she was exaggerating.

"We need to have sex," she said, sweeping her hand down her body. "I'm ovulating."

"How do you know?"

"I peed on a stick thing. And took my temperature. And the app."

I went cross-eyed. "We pee on sticks now?"

"I do, yeah." She nodded. "You don't."

"Oooh," I said, rubbing my temples with both hands. This was a lot of things. We didn't usually use so many things. We just let young love take its natural lusty course. That and wine; wine always helped. Evelyn suddenly, wordlessly, sat up, grabbed the bottom of her blue jumper, and pulled it up over her head, revealing a purple bra.

"What are you doing?" I asked.

Grinning, she balled up the jumper and tossed it onto the floor. "What do you think I'm doing?" She leaned forward, reached her arms around her back, and snapped off her bra, which fell forward onto her stomach.

"I normally take your clothes off."

"Oh," she said, and stopped. "Right."

"There's seduction and stuff. I do my moves."

She let out a deep, mirth-filled laugh, dropped the bra on the floor, and undid the button on her black jeans. "I'm going to meet Sana in an hour. No time for your moves."

"Maybe I wanted your bra on?" I asked, quietly, like a child asking for his ball back.

She let go of her zipper. "I could put it back on?"

I looked back at my monitor. "And I'm busy over here."

She rolled her eyes. "You're not busy, and you've never once refused the chance to have sex with me. So stop playing hard to get and come rrr-ravish me."

"I..." I said, putting my feet down, then putting them back up, because they had become inexplicably heavy. "Well..." I said, confused, because having a stunningly attractive woman topless and come-hithering me wasn't, on the surface, cause for alarm, yet my head was full of sirens.

She beckoned me with her hand. "*Now*. It has to be now."

I stood slowly. "I see," I said, as I knelt onto the bed. She reached across and tried to yank my T-shirt up over my head, but I had clamped my arms to my sides, like a distressed penguin. She leaned forward and wrestled with my T-shirt, knocking off my glasses.

"My moves," I said, fighting her off. "Slow down."

"Sorry," she said, raising her hands. "Let's start again."

"I start," I said, lunging at her and pushing her onto her back. I climbed onto her and we kissed mechanically as she gave up with my top and concentrated on pulling me out of my jeans, which involved as much awkward fumbling as usual, but the kissing was helping and then her hands wandered into my underwear. A minute passed, during which she frowned with increasing intensity when she didn't get the reaction she was expecting. She let go. Not that there was much to hold on to.

"Lie down."

"Where are you going?" I said, but did as instructed.

"Let me help," she said, slipping further down the bed.

"Come back up here. We were kissing."

"Just lie back and relax."

"You're rushing me."

"I'm ovulating."

I closed my eyes. Another minute passed, but I couldn't get into it. "Huh," she said, sitting up on her knees. "That's weird. What's going on?"

I reached for her arm and pulled her towards me. "I just need a minute."

"Okay," she said, lying down next to me, propping her arm under her head. I stroked her back. "This is not like you," she said. "You're very uncomplicated."

"We never needed a schedule before."

"It might have helped, though?" she said. "With getting the timing precisely right?"

"I usually initiate," I said.

Her forehead creased. "You keep track of that stuff?"

"I don't want to be scheduled," I said, and kissed that creased forehead, which felt paternal and didn't help with the overall sexiness of the situation.

"Thing is, though," she said, with a cute little shrug, "I sort of need your sperm."

"Can you ask me more romantically, somehow?"

"Hmm," she said, looking towards the door then back. "I'd love if you'd cum for me, big boy?"

"Oh god," I said, pushing my face into the mattress. We giggled for quite a while, for too long really, since we only had an hour.

"We need a schedule," she said. "I need it to feel like we're doing this seriously. To know that we mean it."

"I'm researching schools," I said, gesturing to my laptop with an open hand. "I have a spreadsheet."

"That's..." She went off in search of delicate wording. "Some weird *you* thing."

"Oh," I said, and thoroughly meant.

"What if you keep the schedule?" she said. "Then you'd be in control."

"Maybe," I said, looking up at the ceiling.

"No," she said, after some more consideration. "Won't work. I need to pee on the ovulation stick and track my temperature and all that stuff. It's always me. My body. I'm the complicated one. Your part is simple. Or has been simple until today."

I lifted the duvet and looked down at my soft, sad, shrivelled penis. "Yes."

"It's never equal," she said. "Man and woman stuff."

"No," I said. "It's never equal."

Her nose twitched. "But then, I want to have a child more than you, so?"

"I don't know if that's true, is it? How would you even quantify something like that?"

"I have less time — that's probably why?"

"Err... no, we have exactly the same amount of time."

She shook her head. "We don't. Not really. You can have a child whenever. You can have a child when you're eighty. Or ten. I have like five years, max."

"I want your child, though." I kissed her on the lips. "I'll homeschool," I said. "Our kid. Deal?"

"Sure," she said, laughing. "Fine."

We lay there for a while, on our backs, until I took a long breath. "Just manage the schedule but never tell me, okay? No calendar stuff. Make it seem like you're just seducing me for your own wicked pleasure. Make it like I've become particularly irresistible, but then also make it seem like it's me doing the seducing, like you're a ripe fruit jiggling on the vine and begging me to pluck you." I channelled all my inner sleaze into my voice. "And you better believe I will pluck you."

Her face cracked. "Ugh," she said, and pulled the duvet up to cover herself. "Never say any of that again, okay?"

"That a no?"

She smiled. "It's a yes. I can do that. That can work."

"I guess," I said, about our sex life, "just because the spontaneity drops, the quality doesn't have to, right?"

For some reason, she found this hilarious.

11

By the end of day two, I was sitting in the hall, gripping my floor mat with both hands, moaning and rocking, as my mind threw great rocks of negativity at me.

You are a failure.
You are failing.
Everyone can do this except you.
Because you suck.
Because you are a failure.
Look at you, failing.
Failure.

When I first met Evelyn, she'd asked me, casually, what memories played on the worst-of reel that looped in my mind's idle moments. This is when I learned that some people have a worst-of reel that loops in their mind's idle moments.

I told her mine was more like a best-of reel.

It wasn't a best-of reel anymore. The scenes playing in it were becoming more negative and upsetting by the hour. Which once again confirmed I'd been wrong about how much control I had of my mind. Which meant I didn't know where it was going to go over the next eight days.

And eight days was a lot of time.

Unless you've done a retreat similar to this one, it's really hard to describe to you in mere words, these humble, small, bent shapes of ink, what twelve hours of nothing, of mechanically following your breath, feels like. All I can suggest is that you try it. That you shut this book, set an alarm for an hour, close your eyes, empty your mind, and focus on your breath entering and leaving your nostrils.

Patiently and persistently even, if that's your bag.

Maybe not for an hour. Try five minutes. That would be a start, but it wouldn't be how it actually felt to be here — because not all seconds, minutes, and hours are made equal. Time dilation is real. An hour spent giggling in the company of your favourite person feels like a minute, while a second with your hand too close to a candle feels like eternity. The first Vipassana meditation hour of day two felt very much like eternity. The second Vipassana meditation hour of day two felt like eternity[2].

The fifth hour — because I'd already forced my body to sit for so long on a cushion and my willpower was long depleted and yet I knew there were still five hours left, and eight days after that — was eternity[3] sitting in a sulphurous hellpit on a chair of spikes being whipped by the devil, who was in a really crabby mood.

While crows pecked out my eyes.

I don't want to seem melodramatic, but throughout the afternoon, I was actually begging for death. I would have bloody loved a bit of death. Would have chosen death, no problem, had it been available in a discreet, painless form, such as a little button I could have pressed or an easy-to-reach cliff — I don't really like hiking or getting muddy — that I could have hurled myself off.

I felt as if my mind were in a vice, and with each deranged mental loop, the handle on that vice cranked tighter. At some point, my mind was going to pop like a grape under the wheels of a speeding monster truck.

I'd come here with a plan — sit for ten tedious days, think about how amazing I was, reflect on how my relationship with Evelyn had fallen apart, go home, fix it, live happily ever after — but as the philosopher Mike Tyson once said, "Everyone has a plan until they get punched in the mouth."

I was being repeatedly punched in the mouth. By my own fist.

I no longer had a plan.

And the only person who could help me was Goenka, who wasn't even a real, living, breathing person, just a too-often-singing recording from 1991 who talked in endless rubbish fables about a world that sounded like 1691 and in which the only people who existed were Householders, Monks, and Housewives. He was also pathologically incapable of getting even close to a point. He was a two-chord song in a genre I didn't like, repeating the chorus "patiently and persistently".

So it's fair to say that when I entered the lecture hall for the second Dhamma Discourse video, I was expecting very little. Our course leader, whom I'd nicknamed Penfold because he resembled the sidekick in the cult 1990s cartoon *Danger Mouse*, was just as pleased to see Goenka as on the previous evening. Goenka's wife was there again, mute. I kept expecting them to give her a newspaper to hold to prove the date.

"Second day," Goenka began. "Slightly better than the first day, slightly better. The difficulties are still there. What a wandering mind. A fleeting mind, a flickering mind. So unstable, so unstable, so infirm. So agitated. No peace, no tranquillity. So wild! Like a wild animal. A monkey mind."

Few people make it this far, he reassured us. In fact, few

even start. He reminded us of the deep cut we'd made to our subconscious. How we'd now tasted much of the pus that would come up. He assured us that no one could harm us more than our own wild mind and that nothing could help us like our mind, trained.

I really wanted to believe him, of course, but the idea that I could train my mind was, at the end of day two, unfathomable. It would have been easier to convince me of levitation or time travel or that AppleFuckFace was a noble, kind person who didn't, I don't know, boil kittens for cheap kicks.

And I was supposed to, somehow, train my monkey mind by just continually interrupting its evil thoughts and guiding it non-judgementally back to the breath? It was like being sent off to break into a Swiss bank vault armed with only a spoon.

I felt as if I'd aged fifty years. Goenka's advice for the pains and aches in my body was simple. "Do nothing. Observe the reality which has manifested itself — an itching has started. See how long it'll last. Any sensation, not going to last forever. It arises and sooner or later passes away. And you are just a silent witness of things that are happening."

By the time the video had ended, I was sobbing. It was the fifth time that day. Why wasn't he talking about what our minds were doing? How they were out for blood, death, and destruction? My mind wasn't a wild monkey — it was a pack of them with power tools hellbent on tearing me limb from limb.

We got up and then the stupid bastard gong sounded and that meant we were supposed to go meditate upstairs some more, but I just couldn't face it. I was a hobbling, hissing mess of anger and confusion and sadness. I ignored the gong and went out to the meadow. The sun was dropping behind the hill and I walked furiously in a perfect square for an hour, maybe even two. The gong went again for lights out. I ignored it and kept walking, flattening the grass with the relentless thud of desperate steps. I promised myself I wouldn't go to bed until I'd figured out why day two had gone so badly. Why it no longer mattered if I was meditating or stomping around out here — because the heckles and trauma-filled loops followed me. There was no respite from them. Why was my mind turning against me? Why did it long for me to suffer?

I'd stay out all night, if I had to.

It went suddenly, bitterly dark. An owl hooted from high in a tree. The moon was fat. I longed to be transformed into a werewolf. It must be a simple life, being a werewolf. Half the day you sleep, the other half you sink your teeth into things, and not in a wishy-washy metaphorical sense. No, you actually just go snap-snap-snapping your long jaw at whatever the hell you want, ripping things, consequence be damned. You fear silver, for some reason.

I'd rip AppleFuckFace's hands clean off. Yeah, that's what I'd do. How would he juggle with no hands? How would he do AcroYoga with no hands? How would he slice the flesh from other people's discarded fruit with...

You get the idea.

The stars were magnificent confetti. These were rural stars, generous and bright and unblemished, like a benevolent child dictator.

For the first time, I considered the possibility of insanity. Not as a lifestyle — although I was sure there was much to recommend about it — but as my present reality.

Why was I going insane? Ah, yes, that was why I was out here. That was what I was supposed to be figuring out. Even the owl had packed up and left by the time I managed to cobble together a theory of what was happening in my head. It might not have been right, but it felt right — had a nice chewy truthiness to it.

This is what I concluded:

The mind is a meaning-making machine.

The better it understands both you and the world, the better it can guide you, the better you'll secure resources and raise your status, the greater the odds you'll find a high-genetic-quality person (or maybe ten) with whom to replicate your genes.

Simple(ish).

When you sit and focus on the breath for twelve hours a day, that meaning-making machine has nothing to do. No inputs are coming in. There is no world to model.

Just as you can't imagine death, it can't imagine not thinking. Not thinking is its death.

When you meditate, you're killing it, best it understands. So it has no choice but to attack you, to make you stop meditating and return it to the sensory theme-park orgy world that it knows. It is relentless. Merciless. It has to be. It will not stop until you open your eyes, stagger up off the mat, and out into the world.

How does it stop you from meditating?

It bombards you with possible thoughts. Imagine a long, winding queue of tiny bubbles. Inside each one is a pre-thought — a topic, memory, idea, fear, random association, sound, lyric, trauma, etc.

The queue is very long. You can't see the back, for it plunges deeply into the twisting, trauma-filled caverns of your subconscious. The front is right there, right beneath your mind's eye.

THINK ME, the pre-thought at the front of the queue begs. *I AM INTERESTING.*

If you agree, that pre-thought grows and grows until it covers your whole mind's eye and you, the Haver of

Thoughts, think it to the momentary exclusion of everything else, most importantly meditation and your stupid breath wheezing in and out.

If you refuse to think it, the bubble disappears, taking that topic, memory, idea, fear, etc. away, momentarily. The queue shuffles forward and the next bubble jumps up and down. *THINK ME. I AM INTERESTING.*

Your job, as a meditator, is to ignore whatever tantalising pre-thought is at the front of the queue at any moment. If you do that, your mind's eye stays blank and you stay meditating.

Hopefully, over time, you get rid of the queue, or learn to ignore whatever is at the front of it, making it easier to just focus on the breath.

On day one, this process had been largely benign. I'd thought of book ideas and new colours and eighties power ballads and random memories. There'd been some heckling, some vivid scenes of Evelyn having wildly enthusiastic sex with better specimens of man than I, but they'd been manageable. Back then, there'd been maybe a thousand different genres of jazzy pre-thoughts bouncing in the queue.

But what I hadn't noticed was that my mind had been testing me. If I successfully ignored a pre-thought, it made a note. That pleasant childhood memory — where I was, I don't know, eight years old and flying a kite through a lavender field in Portugal — wasn't put back in the queue after I'd thought about it.

A pernicious whittling of topics had occurred.

By the morning of day two, the queue was down to twenty-five pre-thoughts that showed promise for distraction; pre-thoughts that had been through the queue and generated an emotional response in me, breaking my focus on the breath.

Now, out here at the end of day two, there were only three pre-thoughts left: the worst of the worst, the most upsetting of the upsetting, the most distracting of all. Goenka wouldn't use the word for them until the next day.

Our demons.

We had to face them.

An epic battle was coming.

And I was going to lose.

12

Day 3/10: AM
Location: Meadow
Mood: Deep foreboding

After an extra-large portion of breakfast porridge — with apples and pears scraped so diligently of their flesh that I held up the queue and ended up eating several seeds — I was ready to start work; the difficult, noble task of understanding myself.

I knew what was happening in my mind now, and while this relaxed me, I still hated what was happening and the lengths to which my mind was willing to go to stop me from meditating and, as a result, make me hate myself.

I was going to meditate.

Today was a new day. A day in which I was going to win and master my monkey mind. I was going to get rid of the queue and ignore the pre-thoughts and not go on any neurotic misadventures into my past. It was only ten hours of silent, patient breath observation (since I was skipping the 4am session). How hard could that really be?

I noticed I was noticing things.

Birdsong at an unusually high pitch.

A cloud that looked like a worm.

Becoming engrossed by the antics of ants gleefully anting.

The soft breeze lifting the hairs on my arms as I walked the path towards that rang alongside the buildings all the way to the meditation hall.

These were only small things, of course, but is life not just small things stacked really high?

That my senses were sharpening gave me a tiny spark of hope that what I was doing here was meaningful.

I sat on my mat and closed my eyes.

In... both nostrils.
Out... left nostril.
In... left nostril.
Out... right nostril.

> Pre-thought: *Hellloooo, I'm a song. Want to hear me?*
> *No. No thank you.*

THINKING
Back to the breath.

In... both nostrils.
Out... left nostril.

> Pre-thought: *Hellloooo, I'm that song again. Want to hear me now?*
> *Are you Kate Bush?*
> *No. Want to hear me?*

No. No thank you. Go away.

THINKING
Back to the breath.

In... both nostrils.
Out... left nostril.
In... left nostril.

Ain't it funny how time slips away?
No. No, thank you. Wait, that's Willie Nelson, right? Is that a song?
Ain't it funny how time slips away? Ain't it funny how time slips away? Ain't it funny how time slips away? Ain't it funny how time slips away? How much time has slipped away from this session?
Please stop. Time isn't slipping away. Time is stuck. Time is broken. Oh, now I've stopped...

THINKING
Back to the breath.

In... both nostrils.
Out... left nostril.

Ain't it funny how time slips away?
No. No, it's not. Shut up.

THINKING
Back to the breath.

Ain't it funny how time slips away? Ain't it funny how time slips away? Ain't it funny how time slips away? Ain't it funny how time slips away? Ain't it funny how time slips away? Ain't it funny how time slips away? Ain't it funny how time slips away? Ain't it funny how time slips away? Ain't it funny how time slips away? Ain't it funny how time slips away?

THINKING
Back to the breath.

In... both nostrils.
Out... left nostril.

Pre-thought: *Here's that time you had your heart broken in a restaurant. Look.*
I don't want to see that. Not interested. No.
Oh, and, ain't it funny how time slips away?

THINKING
Back to the breath.

In... both nostrils.
Out... left nostril.
In... both nostrils.
Out... left nostril.
In... both nostrils.
Out... left nostril.

Pre-thought: *Here's that time you failed your college exams and missed out on university. Ain't it funny how time slips away? Ain't it funny how time slips away?*

THINKING
Back to the breath.

In... both nostrils.

Out... left nostril.
In... both nostrils.
Out... left nostril.

> Pre-thought: *Here's you and Evelyn crying together in a toilet at a house party. Want to watch?*

THINKING
Back to the breath.

In... both nostrils.
Out... left nostril.
In... both nostrils.
Out... left nostril.
In... both nostrils.
Out... left nostril.

> *Ain't it funny how time slips away?*
> *Ain't it funny how time slips away?*
> *Ain't it funny how time slips away?*
> *Ain't it funny how time slips away?*

> Pre-thought: *Here's Evelyn telling you to fuck off in an elevator after her biochemical pregnancy. Look.*

THINKING
Back to the breath.

In... right nostril.
Out... left nostril.

> *Ain't it funny how time slips away?*
> *Ain't it funny how time slips away?*
> *Ain't it funny how time slips away?*

Ain't it funny how time slips away?

Pre-thought: *Here's Evelyn telling you to break up with her. Want to watch?*
Stop. Please.

THINKING
Back to the breath.

In... both nostrils.
Out... left nostril.

Pre-thought: *Here's you being punched by some school bullies while two people you thought were your friends hold you against a brick wall. Want to watch?*

THINKING
Back to the breath.

Pre-thought: *Here's Evelyn having sex with an underwear model. Fun, right?*
I don't want to see that. She isn't doing that. I just want to meditate. I love her. She loves me. Baby or no baby, it will be fine.

THINKING
Back to the breath.

Ain't it funny how time slips away?
Ain't it funny how time slips away?
Ain't it funny how time slips away?
Ain't it funny how time slips away?

Pre-thought: *Here's you breaking your ex-girlfriend's heart.*

You can hear it crack. Listen.

Ain't it funny how time slips away?
Ain't it funny how time slips away?
Ain't it funny how time slips away?
Ain't it funny how time slips away?

THINKING
Back to the breath.

"I CAN'T TAKE IT ANYMORE. I CAN'T TAKE IT. I CAN'T TAKE IT. I CAN'T TAKE IT. I CAN'T TAKE IT," I screamed, into what I thought was my head, but then I noticed the words were actually out my mouth and into the room and, oh no, I was screaming in the meditation hall, and I needed to get away.

I got up and ran out, vaulting down the stairs two at a time. I ran along the path then swerved off it and across the grass into the woods, sobbing giant fat tears.

Ain't it funny how time slips away?
Ain't it funny how time slips away?
Ain't it funny how time slips away?
Ain't it funny how time slips away?
Ain't it funny how time slips away?

I ran faster then threw myself down and screamed some more.

Ain't it funny how time slips away?

I punched the ground.

Ain't it funny how time slips away?

I thumped and thumped and thumped at the dirt, screaming and ranting and raving.

Ain't it funny how time slips away?

I touched my eyes with my muddy fingers. They were

wild, bulbous, and bulging. I touched my mouth: I was grinning — grinning like them, like the volunteers.

My mind had finally snapped.

Ain't it funny how time slips awayAin't it funny how time slips awayAin't it funny how time slips awayAin't it funny how time slips awayAin't it funny how time slips awayAin't it funny how time slips awayAin't it funny how time slips awayAin't it funny how time slips awayAin't it funny how time slips awayAin't it funny how time slips awayAin't it funny how time slips awayAin't it funny how time slips awayAin't it funny how time slips

I began to laugh and let my shoulders relax as I looked down at the craters I'd pounded into the dirt. I held my hands up to the light, admiring their size and the crisscrossing of their veins. I tried to put the dirt back to cover the holes I'd made and grew fascinated by the stunning, rich coppery brown of the soil.

Looking around, I noticed that the colours of everything were tuned up, as if the world were wearing makeup, and I wondered how I'd never noticed how beautiful everything is, and this was, exactly, precisely, the moment that I remembered COLOUR IS A COMPLETE LIE.

A sham.

An illusion.

A practical deceit.

Colour doesn't actually, objectively, exist. It might appear to be a fundamental property of the universe, but it's all just in our heads, created when reflected wavelengths of light hit the cones in our retinas and are transformed into electrical signals that we've learned to interpret as colour. We're the ones who make stars yellow and the sky blue and

—

I looked down and saw a fat, juicy worm crawling over the knobbly root of a large tree.

Middle School. A playground. Adulthood. That scene in Hasenheide Park.

I wanted to splat it.

I hated it.

I loved it.

I felt sorry for it.

It was hilarious to me, this worm, contorting and stretching as tiny hairs I couldn't see helped it grip the ground and slide forward in spasmodic bursts. It was a shit-brown tube.

Its brain had 302 neurons and 7000 synapses while mine had 86 billion neurons and 100 trillion synapses, not that I'm bragging. I knew about hummus and Hamburg and Hiroshima and hieroglyphics and Hegel and habits and haberdashery and hammocks and I could blink, scratch, walk, swim, handstand, talk, write, sarcasm, and orgasm — while it was a shit-brown tube.

Yet, here we were together.

In the same space and time.

And what was I doing with my too-many-to-count advantages, possibilities, and knowledge? Sitting in a room for ten hours, in agony, on a cushion, while my brilliant brain tortured me.

I tipped back my head and howled a primal, deranged, shoulder-shuddering laugh, my wet eyes up to the sky. That laughter split me, and I didn't stop until my stomach hurt and my breath had long abandoned me and I felt sure my shoulders were going to snap free of their sockets and fall to the ground like dead branches.

"Wriggle away, shit-brown tube," I said.

The worm stopped wriggling. The worm turned its

head towards me and reared up like a shoelace-sized snake. "Leave it out mate, will ya?"

I very suddenly grew very still and very cold.

"I'm doing my best, you know? But it ain't easy. You just destroyed my home for starters and there are birds and it's just hard, all right? It's hard being a worm and you're not making it any easier, are you?"

I checked over my shoulder. Everyone was meditating. I wanted someone to confirm what I thought I'd just seen and heard, what I couldn't possibly have seen or heard.

"One day you'll be the food that simple creatures like me eat," it said. Goenka. It had Goenka's voice.

"You're a worm," I said, feeling idiotic while doing so. "You can't talk."

It rose higher still. "Sure about that, dickhead?"

I reached out to touch the worm to confirm that it was a hallucination because, you see, well, a worm was part of one of my demons, but we'll get to that later.

"I think you owe me an apology," the worm said. I lowered my hand.

"I... err... okay. Yeah, I can see why you might think that."

It went quiet.

"So?" the worm asked.

I would not apologise to a worm. I scrambled to my feet and ran off to my room, knowing with certainty that I was a crazed lunatic. The door to my room was closed. I put my hand on its metal handle but found I couldn't lower it because I was afraid to go in. What other things normally silent would now talk to me? My toothbrush, maybe? If toothbrushes could talk, I imagined they'd be very hostile.

I put my ear to the door. There was a sound, a sort of anguished muffled, howl. It didn't have Goenka's voice. It did have Freddie's voice. I opened the door and went in.

Freddie was curled up in the foetal position, facing the wall, rife with his own agonies.

I walked past him and collapsed onto my bed, plunging my head into my pillow, which was when I noticed that my heart was drumming as if I'd just run the full length of a savanna to escape a pride of famished lions.

I was breathing in short gulps and having a heart attack, which was a bit shit. Realising I was having a heart attack only made it worse.

Wait a minute. That's not how heart attacks work.

I remembered a documentary about the heart in which a nurse had said 99 percent of people who call for an ambulance saying they're having a heart attack are having a panic attack.

So I was having a panic attack.

Oh.

It was my first, you see.

It felt as if my soul were being sucked down a narrow drain.

There's madness in my family — enough to scare me — but I'd shown no aptitude for it until this retreat. A worm had just talked to me and that was, I felt, cause for genuine concern.

The monster truck had popped the grape.

I was crazy.

Craziness had arisen.

It would last forever.

Did people go crazy on Vipassana retreats? Have psychotic breaks? If some people went crazy, it would be idiots like me who entered them unprepared, having barely ever meditated, and with no genuine desire to either know or change themselves.

No, wait. Crazy people don't know they're crazy. They think the world is crazy and that they're the only ones making sense. What they see, think, feel, experience *is* real to them, just as colour is real to us — it's just that the map they're using to navigate our shared reality has become corrupted.

They can't rely on it.

It leads them astray.

If I thought I was crazy, I was almost certainly sane. I had lost control of my mind, that was clear, but it wasn't surprising. Not in this environment. The immense stress I'd put on myself. How unprepared I'd been to come here.

With these realisations, my heart rate lowered. I flipped onto my back and began furiously counting the ceiling tiles. There wasn't supposed to be a chapter in my life story in which I was here, on the fringes of insanity, talking to worms. This chapter wasn't supposed to be in the story of Evelyn and me either. Our story had begun as a perfect romantic comedy — two strangers meeting in a bar and then racing each other across India. We used to tell that story often. We hadn't told it in months.

Every couple has a love story. Sometimes those stories go wrong.

Ours began to go wrong in a well-lit room on orange chairs with skinny legs.

13

Berlin, Germany, one year before the retreat

I was at my desk once again, in our shared bedroom, slaving away at the sentence to end all sentences. A sentence that would straighten every ruffle in the universe. A sentence that would unite humanity in all-knowing, wondrous rapture.

Yes! they would shout. *That's it!*

So far, it was just the words *if at first you don't succeed*, but I was optimistic. The sentence to end all sentences was just getting started. I was in no rush to finish it. It was keeping me busy, which was better than sleep-talking into arguments neither of us saw coming, never about the thing, always about the thing.

It had been nearly a year.

Why wasn't it working?

Why wasn't she pregnant?

Why wasn't I as worried about her not being pregnant as she was?

Why could I still be distracted by sentences?

Evelyn appeared, draping herself along the doorframe in the practised, supposedly nonchalant manner she favoured.

In a second, she would pretend to yawn.

She pretended to yawn.

Next, she was going to say *so*, and really drag out the *o*.

"Sooooooo," she said. "How's it going there, then? Hmmm?"

Where were we in the cycle? I couldn't remember.

"You need sperm?" I said, looking from the monitor to her, my hand on my zipper.

"No."

"Cool," I said, turning back to the screen. "Because I'm working on a hell of a sentence, basically."

"Do you know what day it is?" she asked.

"Monday."

"No."

"Tuesday?" What did it matter? Days of the week were just labels. Unlike sentences — sentences mattered. And distractions. Distractions mattered the most.

"Well, I mean, yes, it is Monday," she admitted, nibbling on her bottom lip. "But it's also more than that."

I lifted my fingers from the keyboard. Turned my head. "Your birthday? No. It's not. My... Someone's birthday?"

"It's probably quite a few people's birthday, yes." She rubbed her hands together. "Today is the first anniversary of the Pregnancy Project."

I let out a moan. The name of the project varied. Sometimes we framed it positively (the Fertility Project), sometimes negatively (the Infertility Project, as if infertility were the goal). Sometimes we called it simply the Baby Project. I hated all the names and how this project, no matter its name, had come to dominate our shared life.

"Do you remember what we agreed?" she asked. "In

Hasenheide, that day? My one condition." She walked over and sat on the edge of the bed. Her hands dropped heavily into her lap. "Look at me."

I turned in my chair. We were opposite each other, our knees just thirty centimetres apart. She was doing the thing where she made far too much eye contact because she was afraid she wasn't making enough eye contact.

"It's time," she said, her shoulders lifting just a little.

"Trying already killed our sex life. Is more pressure going to help?"

"Science is going to help."

"It's just..." I stopped. We sat in silence for a while, and then a bit longer. She stared; I looked around her but not at her. I put my head in my hands and did some rubbing.

"Are you going to say something else?" she asked.

"I don't know."

"I hate it when you do that."

"I know."

"We need some kind of signal," she said, trying to be breezy. "We could raise a single finger." She demonstrated.

"I don't always know if I'm going to say something," I said, resisting the urge to laugh. "Often I want to say something else, am planning on it, but then I find there's nothing to say, but I can't admit that to myself because words are supposed to be my thing and so I keep digging hoping to find some."

"It's been a year," she repeated, as if it were an inconvenient but undeniable forensic fact, as if our DNA were all over the crime scene.

"A year isn't that long, is it?"

"I don't have so many years left."

We were thirty-six. "Don't be ridiculous."

"It's not the same for you."

"I know."

"You can leave me in ten years, get a younger girlfriend and have a kid with her. You can have a kid when you're eighty."

"I know."

She shrugged. "So, it's not the same."

"We're not arguing. But I also didn't make it unfair. It's just unfair."

"Yeah, it is," she whispered, lowering her eyes.

"I sort of thought maybe you might be used to it being unfair by now?" I said, and instantly regretted it.

She fell backwards on the bed and cried.

I moved to her and tried to put my arm around her and pull her into my chest, but she fought me off but also not really, not with any gusto. It was awkward, as though we were enemies at a cuddle party, committed to the cause but not each other.

"You're not forty-five," I said, after we'd compromised by lying next to each other, on our backs, holding hands. We talked up to the ceiling.

"It's just, if we do this," I said, weighing every word, "it's a thing. An official thing. We'd be having fertility problems."

"It's already a thing."

"Unofficially, yeah, maybe?"

"It's official for me."

"Not for me, though. I'm still sure it'll work out this month. Or next month, if not."

"Yeah, but you live in your head, not the real world."

"Can't we wait a few more months?"

"We had a deal."

"Yes."

She turned her head towards me. "So?"

"Hmm..." I said.

"I made us an appointment."

My nostrils flared. "What was this conversation about, then?"

"I wanted you to *want* to go there too."

I laughed, but it had an edge. "How's that gone?"

"Not great," she said, and smiled, seemingly against her will. A little of the frost forming between us melted. She moved our hands, still gripping each other, onto her stomach. "This is better than the alternative," she continued. "Which has been us talking about it a lot and it getting bigger and bigger while we don't actually do anything about it. Better just to go. Then we'll see it's really not a big thing."

I noticed my other hand was gripping the bedsheet tightly. "It would be official, though."

"It's already official for me."

We were going round in circles.

"I just never imagined it for us. I was so sure it would work. I'm still sure."

"Optimism is good, to a point."

"It's just not how I imagined our story going," I said.

"No."

"When's the appointment?"

She looked at the bedside clock. "In fifty-eight minutes."

I sat up. "What the —"

"I've already packed everything."

"How far away is the clinic?"

"Forty minutes," she said. "If we take the scooter."

"Is that why you're wearing your shoes?"

"Yes."

"I should have noticed that sooner."

"Yes."

"And your coat."

She shrugged. "You were busy with your sentence."

"Hell of a sentence," I said.

"What you got so far?"

"If at first you don't succeed…"

"Eh," she said, with a kink of her head. She was an excellent kinker, blessed as she was with extraordinary amounts of straw-blonde hair.

"Do I have a choice?" I asked.

"Always."

"Well, that's good then."

An hour and a minute later, they called out Evelyn's name into the waiting room and led us into a swanky office bright enough to do surgery in. Did they do surgery in here? There was certainly a lot of equipment, most of it chrome. I felt as if I'd been beamed onto a spaceship to be probed by an advanced civilisation obsessed with potted succulents.

On the wall to my right was a poster featuring a diagram of the female reproductive cycle entitled "The Miracle of Life." Evelyn and I sat side by side on minimally cushioned orange chairs with skinny metal legs.

"How long have you been failing to conceive?" asked the doctor with a sharp nose and chunky red glasses who sat on the other side of the curved swish desk. She gave us her best dour-German expression.

"A year, to the day," Evelyn said.

The doctor nodded sympathetically. "What have you tried so far?"

Evelyn listed all the things we'd done: the supplements, the apps, the progesterone, the sticks, the whole regime.

"When did you become sexually active?"

"What?" I scoffed. "How does —"

Evelyn answered, unembarrassed.

"Have you ever had an STD?"

"Err…" I stumbled, wondering how the answer might affect not only this process, but also how Evelyn saw me. Had we ever discussed STDs?

It felt as if we were contestants on an exploitative Japanese game show.

The doctor handed us clipboards with thick forms that demanded excessive detail of our sexual histories. I flicked through the pages. There were so many pages. I looked up at Evelyn and she looked back and in both our eyes was panic.

I started writing. Turning pages. Ticking. Listing. Crossing out. Signing. Evelyn had to help me with much of it. My German was good, but this was medical German, only slightly more penetrable than legal German. It's not a cuddly language at the best of times. Little room for romance, ambiguity, padding, denial.

Unfruchtbarkeit

Künstliche Befruchtung

Wechseljahre

Samenspende

"Have you been pregnant before?" the doctor asked, her voice monotone, robotic.

Evelyn shook her head. There was another form.

"Sign here," the doctor said. "And here. Oh, and here."

We stopped reading what we were scribbling on. We just wanted it gone. I'd have signed anything just to get it over with.

"Someone is going to come in and take your blood."

Evelyn nodded. "Okay."

"Okay," I said.

"Not yours," the doctor said, looking at me. "Just your partner's."

"Oh."

The doctor turned back to Evelyn. "And your pulse. And we'll do an examination of your womb."

"Okay."

"And your cervix."

"How regular is your cycle?"

"Regular."

"On a scale of one to ten, how much pain do you experience during your period?"

"I put all this on the form."

"Yes."

"I, well, maybe like a seven?"

"A seven." The doctor nodded once. "And how much pain during sex? How often are you having sex?"

Evelyn turned to me.

I shrugged. "When Evelyn says the app says?"

Ironically, we'd had a lot more sex before we decided to make a human. Our desire for that had decreased our desire for each other, or so an observer would conclude.

A nurse came in with a blood pressure sleeve.

Evelyn turned to me. "Post-hoc rationalise."

"What?"

"Your sentence. If at first you don't succeed, post-hoc rationalise."

I went to laugh but found I'd lost the ability. "A bit too true, maybe?"

She smiled, but it was a weak smile I met with one even tamer. Could we post-hoc rationalise all this failure away if we never managed to conceive a child?

It seemed unlikely.

They led Evelyn to a bed in the opposite corner of the room. To a chair with stirrups.

"And me?" I asked.

"You just sit there," the nurse said.

I let out a nervous laugh. And with this laugh, the reality of our new lives set in — and I realised how unequal those lives would be. Even less equal than they had been. This was all going to happen *to* Evelyn, in her body. The male part, sperm, was almost never the problem. I'd had my sperm checked six months ago because, well, why not? It was the only part I was contributing, and they could check it in a few minutes.

It was fine. It's basically always fine. You need only one winner in an ejaculatory contest with one hundred million participants. To say they've built redundancy into the male reproductive system is not so much stating the obvious — it's climbing to the top of Mount Obvious and screaming, "Men are built for quantity, women for quality."

As they examined Evelyn, I sat with an unexpected feeling: mourning. It had been a year since that day in Hasenheide. Six months since we'd started on the apps and sticks. It had been mourning I'd felt in our bedroom, that day, too. Mourning that we'd lost sex as a frivolous, fun act mostly about itself. Now, I was mourning again — mourning that we were giving control to the Fertility Industrial Complex. That we'd made what was private and vague defined and official. If we weren't careful about how we incorporated this room, this experience, all the invasive tasks it would lead to, into our love story and daily lives, it might come to define us.

Overwhelm us.

Break us.

Our love story had gone wrong.

Would we ever get it back?

14

Day 4/10: AM
Location: Bed
Mood: Loud, howling hopelessness

It wasn't a fitful night's sleep, and the next morning, I awoke with a jolt as the voice inside my head screamed that I was an epic, unrivalled imbecile and wouldn't make it through the day and that everyone who'd ever proclaimed to love me was faking it.

So, yeah, that wasn't great. I could also say with certainty that there were twenty-seven ceiling tiles in my room.

I got up and walked to breakfast.

AppleFuckFace was in the queue, in front of RedHatBoy, GuybrushCreepwood, and BBQedBill. Everyone had a nickname now, and I wasn't out to flatter. If I had a nickname, I suspected it would be AngryWalker, SadEyes, ManWhoStaresAtGhosts, or SobbyMcSobberson.

I ate in furious silence. Fortunately, nothing inanimate came to life and nothing that wasn't supposed to talk talked. My mind was a screen door banging loudly in the breeze.

I went to meditate. During the first session, I found the breath easily enough, I suppose. Ain't it funny how time slips away?

In... right nostril.

Out... right nostril.

In... both nostrils.

Out... left nostril.

I was dreading certain pre-thoughts turning up again and again, but there were only sensations arising to pass away — until I noticed them clustering. Ain't it funny how time slips away? In my body. My lower body. My intimate male area. Ain't it funny how time slips away? There were, how should I put this, eruptions of desire.

Yearnings.

Cravings.

My eyes opened, seemingly of their own volition. A woman in the first row of female meditators, on the other side of the hall, was wearing a tight yellow T-shirt, and if I angled my head like a broken-necked swan, I could see the curve of her left breast.

It was simply exquisite, that breast. Ain't it funny how time slips away? An expression of the highest art and serenest beauty. It was like seeing God herself jiggle. And it promoted the most profound longing within me. My entire body began to quiver with desire.

What was this new devilish trick? My mind was playing my body like a horny fiddle to stop me from meditating. Insatiable lust is just a sensation though, right? Even it must arise to pass away, I reasoned.

Ain't it funny how time slips away?

It got worse. I waited some more. It worsened again.

Why wasn't it passing away? Ain't it funny how time slips away? Well, maybe because sex is unlike anything else. It's the sharp point at the end of the arrow of existence. The desire for it sits deep within the oldest, primal, basal ganglian parts of us. Precisely the parts that are the hardest to ignore. That are the least possible to reason with.

It was quite novel, being horny. When had I last been horny? Not in the previous six months. Not since Evelyn had started demanding I have sex with her because apps and thermometers and ovulation sticks commanded it.

This arousal didn't simply pass away. Instead, as I fidgeted on my mat, it grew stronger and stronger. And it had a soundtrack. Would you like to guess the song?

I threw every curse I had at Willie. I cursed him as though he were the last person at my house party and it was 4am and he was doing a line of coke in the bathroom and trying to convince my girlfriend to have a threesome.

A threesome.

A twosome.

Even a onesome would have been fine. Ain't it funny how time slips away? Well, time was doing no such thing. I sat on my sweat-drenched cushion being waterboarded by arousal. And this was only the first meditation session of the day. By the second, the craving was ten times as consuming and I was biting chunks out of my cheek. It wasn't only women now. The man in front of me had long, hair — the default hairstyle here — and broad, sculpted shoulders and I thought, well, if I shut my eyes as I caressed him, would it really matter? There was still much beauty there to enjoy, regardless of his inconvenient (for me) outie-rather-than-innie genitalia.

Full disclosure: these thoughts weren't entirely new. Back on day two, I'd noticed that I was finding the other male meditators increasingly yummy. In the beginning, I'd felt they had too much gristle on their hungry lumberjack bones, that I could smell stinky vegan righteousness wafting off them. Paddle-boarders, many of them, I suspected. People who owned essential oils. These oils had to be incorrectly named because I didn't own any and I was still here, existing, sometimes even flourishing.

Had been for years.

Nearly forty of them.

I've wandered off-topic.

Men. I guess that was the topic. Men can be hot too, basically.

I closed my eyes again.

This must be what it's like in prison, I thought. You make do. You adjust. Nature finds a way. Jeff Goldblum had told me as much, when I was too young to understand what a dog whistle was.

I really, really, really wanted to have sex.

Be touched.

Kiss a shoulder.

Any shoulder.

Even my own shoulder.

Tongue a clavicle.

I'd been whipped into a frothy frenzy of lust. They'd warned us about this at the start, in the pamphlet, but I hadn't known it would be this bad. Hadn't known that all my body's blood would pool in my groin. It was simply impossible to meditate in this state. The queue was very, very long but each pre-thought was the same: *SEX!!!!!!!!!*

So, yeah, I wasn't meditating, and I was growing surer that everyone around me was further along the yellow brick road to enlightenment. Skipping off into the distance. Was I still on the road? I seemed to have swerved off, was becoming entangled in long, sticky, seedy weeds.

Eventually, the session ended, but I wasn't sure how to

leave the room because I had a significant erection problem. I was fourteen again. I had no desire to be fourteen again. That had been a difficult time because I'd been as possessed by lust as that girl in *The Exorcist* was by curses. There was basically nothing else in my life for about a year. Just SEX!!!!!!! and maybe sherbet.

My fellow meditators left the room. I kept my eyes screwed shut, pretending I was pious and doing a little overtime with the Big Nothing. There was a baggy jumper in my room. I needed to get to my room. But I had to cool off first. I tried to focus on my breathing but that was a wash, so I devoted several careful minutes to thinking about the intricacies of the nine times table, and when that didn't work, I thought about golf.

Because there's nothing on this formerly green earth that I detest more than golf. It's a hatred that I developed during that month in Bangkok — a giant exhaust pipe of a city. While out one day doing elaborate nothing, riding the SkyTrain, I saw a glorious, enormous, virgin expanse of pristine green.

Wonderful, I'd thought. I'd get off at the next stop and pass an afternoon on it, stubbornly horizontal, an ice cream in one hand, a book in the other, surreptitiously watching grannies do tai chi.

I squinted because I'd seen a shape on that green.

No, two shapes.

Tiny shapes. They had large bags, the shapes.

Golfers!

All that space, all that prime, juicy, unreal real estate was actually private land, fenced and patrolled and reserved for the occasional post-work jolly of a handful of rich men knocking their tiny balls around. Golf is the least effective use of space ever devised by humanity. It is so flagrantly, arrogantly wasteful that it simply must be, deliberately, so.

Golf is bad by design. Which is why golf clubs must charge so much. Which is what gives the few idiots who play it the social status they desperately crave.

The only good thing about golf is that when I'm thinking about golf, I'm too incensed to think about sex. And so — albeit with my mind's screen door banging ever harder in the breeze, hitting golf, men's shoulders, and Jeff Goldblum — I was able to get out of the meditation hall without being arrested.

As I plodded down the corridor to my room, muttering to myself, one of the volunteers — the one who had checked me in, YoungUriGellar — approached me.

"Are you okay?" he asked.

Never better, I said, in my head. He didn't react to that, of course, because he wasn't in my head, so I decided I'd better change strategy or this conversation would go nowhere fast. "Never better," I said, with my mouth, which was weird because I didn't talk with my mouth anymore, except to myself. And a worm, once. The words were all lumpy and slow.

"You're talking to yourself," he said.

"Am I?"

"Yes."

"It's part of my process," I said, which was a very grandiose term for falling apart, but there we were.

"Do you need some time with the course leader?" he asked.

"Later, maybe," I said, and he nodded and walked away and I went to my room and scooped up my jumper and was annoyed that he'd make me speak and annoyed that he'd noticed I was struggling and annoyed that I'd not answered truthfully and all that annoyance was like a heavy rock I huffed out to the woods and tried to throw off in a scrubby clearing while some birds sang and a caterpillar stared at me and I think also judged me and found me lacking.

I saw a particularly attractive tree.

Sturdy.

Proud.

Hard.

Ancient.

I became engorged again and looked around in panic. I thought about running deeper into the woods, but there were too many people in there now. Weird people like me — crying, hiding, howling, punching, erect. It was becoming like a Japanese suicide forest where you didn't know exactly what you'd find in the next clearing but whatever it was was almost certain to ruin your day.

I darted back towards my room, hiding in the shadows and corners, behind bushes and walls, mumbling to myself like a sad pervert. The throbbing continued unabated. The need was overwhelming and urgent. If Freddie was out, I'd masturbate. There was simply no alternative course of action, rules be damned.

I opened the door.

Freddie was out.

Eureka.

I sat on my bed, my hand massaging my thigh. Masturbation was against the rules, of course — an act of sexual impurity, Goenka called it — but it was also the only way out of this misery. The only way I could calm my mind and body and get back to the breath, back to my demons, back to progress and the fading dream of greater self-understanding.

Maybe this was an essential part of it, this ruinous horniness? Maybe I would progress to the next step if I gave in to it?

I was torn. My hand wandered closer to my groin, caressing as it moved. I pulled it back. It wandered again. I held it down with my other hand and bit my lip so hard there was blood.

Freddie came in. Saved me. He had an erection, too. The gong sounded. It was only mid-morning. There were so many more hours to get both crazier and more titillated.

Hang on?

The hat he was wearing.

I peered around the wooden divider. A black hat with the word D$GE on it. Where had I seen one like it before?

15

Berlin, Germany, three months before the retreat

Evelyn and I were standing in the crowded kitchen of a house party of a colleague or a friend or a friend's colleague and this person was almost certainly called Sam, or Sandy, or Simone.

There was an S for sure.

The narrow, L-shaped kitchen had 70 percent of the party crammed within it, as dictated by German House Party Law. I coughed into the nearest cloud of smoke as tight pockets of humans poured each other drinks and shouted the anecdotes of their lives into the ears of strangers almost certainly called Sam, or Sandy, or Simone.

There was an S for sure.

Evelyn was next to me but looking as if she'd rather be anywhere else, even her own funeral, tipping a wine bottle up to the light. Neither of us had wanted to come here while both agreeing that we needed to come here. That this would be a better use of our Saturday night than another evening on the couch numbing ourselves with the movies of Nicolas Cage.

Three rounds of artificial insemination, high doses of a cocktail of assorted fertility meds, wildly changeable moods. Evelyn wasn't able to think about anything else; I was hiding in anything else.

I wasn't even sure I cared if it worked anymore. I just wanted it over.

"So where did you two meet?" a man who worked with existential angst, no, wait, existential risk said. "Let me guess — Tinder?"

"Not Tinder," I said, chucking back the last of my Beck's. If Evelyn was listening, she was hiding it well. I glanced back at her. She was on her tiptoes, looking over my shoulder, towards the window, perhaps searching for a glass that fewer than ten people had slobbered into.

"Bumble?" he tried.

"Evelyn?" I said, turning around. "This nice computer man is asking where we met. Hell of a story, right?" I pretended to turn the throttle of a tuk-tuk.

"Hmm," she said.

I beckoned her into the small space between me and this modern-day superhero saving humanity one thwarted neural network at a time. "You start."

She looked at the space, frowned, didn't move. "We met in a bar," she said. "Like how everyone used to meet." She lifted the wine bottle and tipped the rest of its contents down her throat.

Weird. She shouldn't be drinking. She'd told me the data, that alcohol had a small but not quite inconsequential effect on fertility. And all we were able to tweak were the small but not quite inconsequential things.

She walked out to the hallway as the song changed, and

I had to disagree — love wasn't going to tear us apart. Infertility was.

"How long before AI enslaves us?" I asked the nerd.

"It won't with me around."

"Oh, that's a shame."

Evelyn and I had learned over the past year and a half that wanting a child isn't like wanting other things. If you really want a particular job but don't get that job, you can take another job. It won't be the same job, but it won't be that different either — e-mails, bosses, meetings, meetings that should have been e-mails.

If you really want a particular apartment but don't get that apartment, you can take another apartment. It won't be the same apartment, might have worse light or be further from your favourite Indian restaurant, but it won't be that different either — toilet, kitchen, shower, ceiling, doors.

And so on.

But if you really want a child but can't have a child, you… get a dog?

Or adopt, maybe? Germany has the second-lowest fertility rate in the developed world. There's a shortage of children, not a surplus. You could foster, for a time, maybe, but with the caveat that the child you will grow to love might be taken from you again. Evelyn's sister had looked into it during the six years she and her partner had spent trying to conceive.

Six years.

We wouldn't make it six years.

Ten minutes later, Evelyn hadn't returned. I went looking for her. The apartment had four large rooms, but only the kitchen and the living room had hit a critical mass of revelry, had their own centres of gravity. I checked the living room, but it hadn't ensnared her. I opened the front door. Her faithful, strappy black shoes were still out there hugging the hallway wall, swarmed by the shoes of later arrivals.

I knocked on the bathroom door. "Evelyn?"

"*Besetzt*," she said. Busy.

"It's me."

"Go away."

I put my ear to the door. I thought I heard crying, but the music and conversation and laughter — what could really be so funny? — was too loud.

I knocked again. "It's me."

A woman appeared behind me. "Someone in there?"

The door opened. I slipped inside.

"Hey," the woman said.

"We'll be quick."

"Use a bed. That room's em —"

I locked the door behind me. Evelyn was sitting on the side of the bath, her cheeks wet and mascara running.

"Blood," she said, and I knew what that meant. Another sad cycle had come to its end. "It's too much," she said, and her eyes screwed closed and she let out an anguished howl. I got her some toilet paper so she could blow her nose and blot away the mascara. "The waiting. The buildup. The crash. I can't do this." Her voice cracked. "It's killing me. It's all I think about. But I can't make the days pass quicker. I just want the time to pass. This is the worst phase of my life."

I burst into tears with a speed and ferocity that shocked us both. We were supposed to be the best phase of each other's lives. We were so far from the script my mind had written for us that I no longer even knew the genre of our lives. It certainly wasn't a romantic comedy anymore. Had it become a tragedy?

A knock on the door. "Come out!"

"One second," I shouted, irritated, wiping my eyes. "Can we leave?" I asked.

"It was you who wanted to come."

"Was it? Well, now I want to leave."

"I can drink now, though," she said.

A fist on the door. "HURRY UP."

This reminded me of something. A breakup, maybe?

"You were already drinking," I said.

"I could feel it coming," she said.

"I wasn't judging you."

"Let's stay," she said. "Get drunk. Dance. When did we last dance together?"

We used to dance often, in the Before Times. The Before Times were easy; weightless. I unlocked the door, which flew open, knocking into my foot.

"I'M GOING TO PEE MYSELF," the woman said, blowing past me and to the toilet, where she pulled her underwear down from beneath her skirt. She was squatting before we'd even left. The door was still open.

I didn't feel like dancing.

We went to the kitchen and pulled two more bottles of Beck's from the fridge. You could enter the room only sideways now, feeling like a Tetris block, apologising profusely as you turned and turned, trying to fit. The kitchen had 85 percent of the party, was overpowering the living room, was going to swallow us all unless we resisted.

We resisted, forcing our way back out and towards the bathroom then moved into a bedroom, empty but for a man in a black D$GE hat, who had collapsed on the same yellow IKEA chair we had at home, his eyes rolled up into his head.

Drugs, basically.

"This Stacey's room?" I asked, noticing someone

vaguely familiar in the photos dotting the frame of the mirror.

"Sana."

"Right."

"Looks like our bedroom a bit. Isn't this your rug?"

"All apartments in Berlin look the same." Her shoulders sagged. "We're all the same."

We sat side by side on the bed, our shoulders lightly touching. I guzzled my beer. "What if we took a break?"

She jerked her head back. "We can't take a break."

"But you just said you can't do it anymore?"

"Of course we're not going to take a break." Her voice rose. "What a ridiculous thing to say. How would taking a break help?"

"I thought it's what you wanted?"

"What do you want?" she said, and tutted. "Don't just say things."

I rubbed my head. "I want you to not suffer."

"That's not an option right now," she said, quietly.

The sounds of the kitchen mixed with the old-school hip-hop beats of RUN-DMC, brave for a party this white. You used to be able to tell when things were being enjoyed ironically. The world might not quite be post-truth, but it sure felt as though it were post-irony.

We sat silently while I thought about what I wanted. It was like picking from a menu of advanced interrogation techniques. Even if some were preferable to others — even if being stress-positioned was better than having my testicles electrocuted — it was all torture.

If we couldn't take a break, then what I wanted, more than to watch *Face/Off*, even, was for it to be Monday morning. For it to be 8am so that she would kiss me on the cheek and wish me a nice day and leave me the hell alone for ten hours so I could be with all my various hard-won, stress-tested tools of distraction.

I could tell her I had an event to go to on Monday night. Yes. That was Monday done. Then it would be Tuesday. Then it would be 8am and she'd kiss me on the cheek and wish me a nice day and leave me the hell alone for ten hours so I could be with all my various hard-won, stress-tested tools of distraction.

On Tuesday I usually played football. Then it would be Wednesday.

I wanted to not look at her face — a face I hadn't been able to stop looking at during the first blissful year of our love. I didn't want to see how sad and serious and chewed up and spat out and chewed back up and spat back out again it had become. But you can't tell your partner that and so I said, "What I'd like, I think, maybe, is a ban on talking about the Pregnancy Project for a while. Like, we do the things, the appointments and stuff. But that's it. We pretend it's not happening?"

She tutted again. "When has not talking about things ever helped anyone?"

"It helps," I said, defensively.

"I talk about everything."

"We've given it too much focus and attention."

"It's LITERALLY all I think about. It's on a constant loop. It never ends. Never stops. I don't know why. Why therapy and support groups and house parties and stupid Nicolas Cage movies don't fix it. But they don't fix it."

I tried to put my arm around her, but she pushed me away. "It's like a virus has infected my brain. Do you know what that's like? To live like that?"

I chugged the last third of my beer then burped. "Nope."

"I can't believe I've done this to us."

I sighed. "We both agreed to it."

"When IVF doesn't work, you need to leave me."

"I'm not going to leave you. Don't be ridiculous." I looked across at D$GE, but he was still up there, floating in space.

"I'll leave you," she said.

"Don't say things like that."

"I can't be the reason you don't have a family. I can't live with that kind of guilt."

"We still have IVF," I said.

"That's 32 percent, at best. And we can only afford three cycles. If we make it that long." She squeezed her eyes shut. "And I'm stuck in a job I hate but can't change because I have no idea if this will ever work and you don't change jobs when you're pregnant. My life is just a tragic limbo."

"It'll work next month." I stood. "Let's go. I don't want anyone else to see us like this."

She put down her beer on the floor and stood as well. "I don't even want us to see us like this."

16

I had to admit it. YoungUriGellar was right. I needed help. I remembered that the pamphlet had said we could book brief sessions with Penfold, if needed, and it had emphasised the *need* part strongly. I didn't ask for help easily. It was part of why Evelyn had sent me here, so the fact I was willing to see him told me I probably needed to. The last two days had been so rough I felt as if I'd gone down with the *Titanic* only to be rescued by the *Hindenburg*.

Ain't it funny how time slips away? Ain't it funny how time slips away? Ain't it funny how time slips away? Ain't it funny how time slips away?

I went to the lower level of the meditation hall. Outside the Dhamma Discourse room, I sat on a bench full of people, all eyes downcast. There was a manic edge to the air. AppleFuckFace was there, three people ahead of me. While we waited, I threw sharp mental daggers at him. I was happy that he was failing, too. I was sure his mind was a swirling necropolis of unmentionables.

Ain't it funny how time slips away?
Ain't it funny how time slips away?
Ain't it funny how time slips away?

Ain't it funny how time slips away?

He wasn't in the room long. Probably Penfold told him his soul was stained beyond any possibility of cleansing. Three people later, the door opened and RockBandAccountant left, which meant I was free to enter. My stomach was fluttering. Inside the room, I found Penfold sat in the middle of a small stage, on a cushion, in the lotus position. That most wholesome position of them all. The one that said *Comfort? I've transcended it.*

YoungUriGellar gestured for me to sit in front of Penfold, on the hard floor. The room reeked of incense. There was a framed picture of Goenka on my right. I hissed at it with my mind, as if I were a territorial goose. I squatted, roughly twisting my legs under me, ending up in only the sloppiest of lotuses.

AintitfunnyhowtimeslipsAintitfunnyhowtimeslipsAintitfunnyhowtimeslips

Penfold pressed his thin, token-gesture lips together then nodded ever so slightly.

AINTITFUNNY

"I — I'm... not doing very well," I said, surprised by how quietly my words came out. I cleared my throat.

... how time slips away?

"What makes you think you aren't doing well?" he asked.

"I'm getting stuck in constant loops. Very negative loops. Violent ones. And also a song lyric. It's stuck."

... how time slips away?

"Saṅkhāras," Penfold said knowingly, his head tilting backwards. Goenka talked often of saṅkhāras, believing everything was either a cycle of craving or aversion.

"Yes," I said, "well, I mean, maybe? Is everything a saṅkhāra?" I asked, with a tone that hinted that I didn't think you should reduce the entirety of human experience to a simple binary choice, as if we were just magnets wandering around either repelling or attracting.

"Yes," he said, calmly. So, so calmly.

"Even... like... love?"

Ain't it funny how time slips away?

Ain't it funny how time slips away?

Ain't it funny how time slips away?

He laughed, just a little, as if love were a passing fad. As if love were Bulletproof coffee and flaxseed-oil smoothies and fidget spinners and Peloton bicycles. "Some Buddhist scholars have quantified and recorded all human emotions. Love is in there too. I forget its number in the table."

"That's..." I lowered my eyes. "Really, really sad. How do I get past them?" I said, my eyes snapping up. "My demons. I know them all. They're... old. I'm... I think I'm facing them? I talked to a —"

I stopped because I was babbling, and also because I didn't think it was a good idea to tell him the worm had talked back.

"It's about accepting," he said. "Not defeating. Try not to think of it as a battle."

"What else could it be?"

"It's Vipassana," he said, and let one of those wide, self-satisfied smirks rip across his face. YoungUriGellar, who was sitting just behind him, rang an infinitesimally small gold bell, as if he were an aristocrat summoning a servant to bring him a cucumber sandwich — without crusts.

"That's it?" I said, incredulous. The door opened. GuybrushCreepwood stepped in. Why hadn't he waited for me to leave? I tried to get up, but apparently my legs weren't working. "Wait," I said. "The demons. I need to know how to —"

"That concludes the session," said Penfold.

AIN'T IT FUNNY

I
N
'
T
IT
T
FUNNY
U
N
N
Y
HOW
O
W
TIME
I
M
E
SLIPS
L
I
P
S
AWAY
W
A
Y
?

"But," I said, in a high-pitched whine, because they hadn't helped me at all, the insufferable cretins. YoungUri-Gellar rose to his feet and ushered me towards the door. I stumbled out, knocking into GuybrushCreepwood's shoulder as I passed.

In a hell of a strop, I stormed towards my room. Why

had I thought he'd be able to help me, anyway? As I walked, focusing on the ground, muttering gibberish, singing a particular line from a particular song, I stopped abruptly. Ants were blocking the path, spilling out from beneath a bush I didn't know the name of because I don't know the names of any bushes because I'm a buffoon.

"Get out of my way, ants," I said to the ants, which were in my way. The ants didn't move. "Don't fuck with me, ants," I said, more loudly, to the ants that were still very much in my way. They were running from the grass on my left across the path carrying some kind of green leaves and then disappearing under the bush growing next to the building and into their home, I supposed.

I remembered the rule about not killing anything and I thought how much breaking that rule might hurt Penfold and Goenka and I got quite warm and fuzzy inside and lifted my flip-flop above a cluster of these scurrying, industrious ants, and then slammed my foot down, instantly killing four, or maybe even five of them DEAD.

As I committed this sin — sorry, I mean this saṅkhāra of aversion (to ants and rules and this retreat), no, wait, saṅkhāra of craving (to hurt Goenka and Penfold and myself?) — I heard something. It was quiet, but it was also, unmistakably, conversation.

Human conversation!

Staying low, I peered around the edge of the building. I was at the corner of the accommodation block reserved for returning meditators, like GingerCircusBear. Often the doors were open and I could get a glimpse of these seasoned sufferers lying on the hard, unforgiving ground looking sad and superfluous, like unemployed poltergeists in a poltergeisting recession.

Perhaps five metres away, at the door to the building, two men were talking. One was facing me, holding the door open with his shoulder, which was kind of flabby — the bald man with inflamed skin I'd compassionately nicknamed BBQedBill. The other had long hair in a ponytail and —

Wait a second. That blue T-shirt, that frame, those delts.

He turned. Yes, it was him. *AppleFuckFace!*

I dropped lower onto my haunches, not wanting them to see me. The bush and four, or maybe even five dead ants obscured me. I strained to hear, but their despicable treachery was too quiet. They knew what they were doing was wrong.

They continued talking. I licked my lips and was sure that I could taste chocolate ice cream and a million euros and unicorn sperm.

I could tell on them. My revenge. *Yes.* I could get them in a whole heap of trouble. And why shouldn't I? Their obviously unequanimous minds had succumbed to fraternising in public and so threatened the hard, diligent work of us fellow enlightenment seekers.

I remembered that I'd just killed four, or maybe even five ants out of nothing but misdirected petty vengeance. And that yesterday, I'd taken three sessions off to count ceiling tiles. Was I really better than they were? They were probably just doing their best, weren't they?

A distant voice answered me, full of echo, as if from the back of a cave: *Weren't you doing your best, Adam, when you sliced that apple?*

"Nnnn-yes?" I said, to this distant voice. I stood up, about-turned, and marched back to the meditation hall. Penfold's pointlessly brief non-help sessions were over, but I found YoungUriGellar sweeping the vestibule. He had his back to me. I stood close to him but didn't make a noise because I wasn't allowed to make a noise. He continued to sweep. I cleared my throat. He turned.

"People are talking," I said, without making eye contact. "At the entrance to the next accommodation block."

"Who?" he asked.

"BBQ" — I remembered that this was a personal nickname — "blue T-shirt and ponytail. Red T-shirt and bald."

He passed me his broom and scampered away. Would they still be talking? I looked down at the broom. Had he given it to me with the expectation I would broom for him?

I broomed for no man.

I leaned the broom against the wall, sat down, and waited.

What was Evelyn doing out there in the real world? I wondered. Was she hunched over her laptop, frantically searching for some fresh fertility science? Was her mind as out of control as...

Wait a second. I remembered the house party, how she'd told me that the thoughts in her mind were like a virus. How they infected her and never stopped, no matter what she did. She'd asked me if I knew what that was like. And what had I said?

Nope.

I had said, simply, "Nope". I hadn't even lied to make her feel less alone and crazy.

It was like this.

It was exactly like this.

Exactly like what my mind was doing to me. She had been here, where I was now. She had lost control of her mind. That virus had taken it over. I let out a loud howl and cried into my hands. I'd been like this for only three days. She'd lived like this for months.

No wonder she'd looked so haunted.

It's torture to lose control of your mind, and I hadn't helped her, not really. I just hadn't understood. Thought I could distract her and when that didn't work, when I decided I was just making things worse, I avoided her. I should have forced her to make me understand. Should have climbed into her head. Gone with her to meet her demons, as she would have done for me. I was here because she was trying to help me.

I suddenly remembered many times where I could have been a much better partner: That party. When I'd created all those pretend deadlines. When she'd challenged the doctor with all those articles. The second opinion.

I kicked the broom. It clattered to the floor. I needed to get back to her. I needed to apologise. To tell her I understood now. That I had been there too.

17

Berlin, Germany, one month before the retreat

I was making my breakfast in the kitchen when I heard the scream. I ran to the bathroom.

"It worked?" she said, looking up at me from her perch on the toilet. "Did it work?"

I squinted down at the display on the pregnancy test — two pink lines, sort of, just about, maybe.

"No way," I said, jumping up and down. "It worked?"

She yanked it back towards her. "We need more light."

We ran into the hallway and she tilted the test back and forth under the circular spotlights near the mirror she used to do her makeup.

"They never do this in the movies," I said. The control line, near the C, was thick and vibrant while the test line, near the T, was faint.

"You see it too, though, right? The second line?" she said. "I'm not crazy?"

I took it from her again. "Should it be so faint?"

"I don't know," she said, reading the instructions for the

twenty-fifth time. "It says nothing about faint lines. Shit. I'm panicking. We need to google, right now. You do English and I'll take German. We meet back here in fifteen minutes. *Go.*" She was on the move before she'd finished the sentence.

We ran for our laptops, hers on the couch and mine at my desk. I could hear my heart in my ears. Was it finally over? The relief was palpable, like a tight hug. Five minutes of frantic googling later, I went to find her.

"Internet says there's no such thing as a faint line."

She shut her laptop, grinning. "German says the same. No false positives. There are no false positives." She waved her hand in front of her face. "I'm pregnant. Oh, my god. Tissues. Give me tissues."

I jumped over the side of the couch and fell onto her and we wept all over each other and were quickly a gooey, sticky mess. "Fuck."

"Fuck."

"I love you," I said, kissing her wet lips, salty with tears.

"I love you more."

"We did it?"

She blew out air. "WE DID IT."

"Do we have more tests?"

She laughed and grabbed my hand and pulled me into the bathroom and opened her medical drawer. There were dozens of them in a heap next to all her various fertility medications. "I need to call the clinic," she said. "After we do, like, ten more tests."

Two hours later we were sitting in the waiting room, in our usual seats. This time, though, my arm was around her shoulder. Behind the desk was a stack of success boxes that the staff gave to couples who became pregnant. They contained nappies samples and a rattle and... well... I didn't know, actually, because they'd never given us one. We often made fun of those boxes, how ridiculous they were, how little that stuff would matter to a couple finally pregnant and free of this place, after months or years of expensive false starts. What they really needed were commiseration boxes they gave out at the end of each failed cycle.

"I want the box," I said. "It's not official until we get the box."

They called us in. It was the same office in which we'd had our first appointment. The "Miracle of Life" poster. The same dour doctor, the same chunky red glasses, the same poker face. The doctor took Evelyn's blood and measured the levels of her HCG, the pregnancy hormone. We held hands under the desk. They sent us out, they called us in again. The doctor's mouth was narrow and tight rather than wide and relaxed. The wrong kind of mouth.

"Your HCG levels are very low," she said. "We'd like to see them a little higher."

Evelyn let out a yelp.

"No," I said.

"They need to be doubling every two days," the doctor continued. "The trajectory is what matters. Come back in two days and we'll test again."

"Two days?" Evelyn said, as if it were two months. The doctor tried to smile but it was a shoddy effort. "Then we'll know for sure."

We left boxless.

"Two days," Evelyn said, in the elevator. "What are we going to do for two days?"

"Suffer?"

"Do you know what to feel?" she asked.

"Not a clue."

"I'm going to just not," she said, her arms wrapped across her chest. I didn't believe her.

"Shall we go for lunch? There's that—"

"I need to consult the scientific literature."

"That's what the clinic is for, my love. That's their job."

"They don't care," she said. "Not like I care."

Two days and twenty-five tests later, the last five of which had been negative, we went back to the clinic for news we knew would be bad.

"So, this was what we call a biochemical pregnancy," the doctor said.

"I know what they are," Evelyn said.

"Honestly," the doctor continued, "if the tests hadn't become so sensitive, most of these wouldn't even register. That would be better."

"I'm not pregnant," Evelyn repeated, almost as a question.

"We'll go again next month," the doctor said. "Not to worry."

"Not to worry?" she said, her voice cracking. "My eggs are obviously rubbish. Why wouldn't we worry?"

"Everyone at the clinic is very optimistic about a positive outcome. It's just going to take time." The doctor opened a drawer in her desk. "Look, in the meantime, many of our patients talk highly of acupuncture. For stress relief. We have a special program." She rummaged, looking for a flyer.

"Acupuncture?" Evelyn asked, as if she'd been offered an on-fire camel. "Acupuncture?! What kind of place is this?" She looked around, as if she'd just arrived. "We come here for science. Serious fertility science."

"Right," said the doctor, shutting the drawer and glancing up at her monitor. If there were a panic button, she'd have been reaching for it. She cleared her throat, pressed both her palms onto the desk. "Well, I guess what I'm trying to say is it's important to think about your physical *and* mental health."

"She's right," I said, reaching for Evelyn's hand. "This is taking a lot out of you."

Evelyn turned and flashed her teeth. I fell back into my seat. She was usually so calm and respectful. She didn't make scenes with strangers.

"Your chances really are very good," the doctor said, lifting her hands and bringing them together. "I'm extremely confident of a positive outcome."

"When?" Evelyn asked.

"Err, well, obviously, we can't know when, exactly."

"Thanks for your time, Doctor," I said, getting up. "We're going to go home and regroup and then do another artificial insemination round—"

"Sit down," Evelyn growled. I froze halfway between sitting and standing.

"O-Okay," I said, sitting back down.

"I can't drag this out anymore," Evelyn said. "It's killing me. We fire the nukes. *IVF*. As soon as possible. Well, I mean the ultra-long protocol with Lupron Depot injections, so three months of downregulation first, right? Would that be your opinion, too?"

The doctor's eyes shrank to half their normal size. "The ultra-long protocol? Three months? Who said anything —"

"Because of my adenomyosis."

The doctor tapped on her computer. "That's not done here."

"In this clinic?" Evelyn challenged.

"In Germany."

The doctor pushed the mouse away. Evelyn rummaged in the backpack at her feet and pulled out a stack of neatly stapled, highlighted, sticky-noted articles from scientific journals. She dropped them with a thud onto the desk.

"I've done a quick read of the scientific literature. In the

US, they're way ahead on this stuff and some of the most-recent research is —"

The doctor slid slowly back from her desk, as if she were on a bad date and he'd started talking about dollar-cost averaging his index funds.

I reached for Evelyn's hand again. "Let's take some time," I said, in English. "To collect ourselves. This has been a lot."

The sudden blast of English threw Evelyn off her stride. She powered down and put her hands on her lap but then seemed to whir back to life.

"I'm not saying it's unanimous, but the literature is clear — it's better to follow the ultra-long protocol. Three months of suppression, let the adenomyosis clear up, and then do the implantation when the scarring will be minimal, assuming there are any eggs in my body worth a damn."

"We have a lot of experience," the doctor said, scraping her bottom lip against her teeth. "And that would be overkill."

"What I've read says otherwise."

"I don't know what you've read."

Evelyn pointed to the stack of papers. "It's all here."

"We follow the literature. We're professionals. And we have the highest success rate of any clinic in Germany. It's why you're here."

Evelyn tutted. "I feel like I'm not being listened to."

Underneath the window, a tram trundled past, and I really wanted to be on it.

"If IVF had failed five times already," the doctor said, cautiously, "it's an avenue we could explore."

"I want a second opinion," Evelyn said, turning to me. "We want a second opinion, don't we?"

I startled. I wasn't used to being asked. Or asking. Whether or not I agreed with Evelyn, I had to live with

Evelyn. I wasn't sure if she was right, or if that even mattered. Was this not about her finding some way to take control? To not be a passive victim in all of this? But if she was wrong, this would delay us for at least three months. Would we last three more months?

"Erm... yes?" I said, while squirming and not meeting anyone's eyes.

"I can ask another doctor —"

"From a different clinic," Evelyn said, interrupting the doctor and reaching for her stack of articles. "I'll need a copy of all our results."

We left boxless again.

"What was that?" I asked, in the elevator, pressing the button for the ground floor. "That shit was right out of *A Beautiful Mind*. You can't use that many sticky notes. It freaks people out."

The door closed. "She should be more up to date with the scientific literature. And you could have backed me up more. You're just a sucker for anyone in authority."

"Me? Seriously. That couldn't be less true. Do you think maybe you might be losing it?" I said, as the door opened.

She flashed her teeth again, her eyes pinpricks of fury. "You don't get to say that to me." She stomped out to the street.

"Everyone we talk to says our chances are good," I said, running after her. It was raining lightly.

"They're paid to say that," she said. "Did you see how she just dismissed the biochemical pregnancy as if it were nothing? As if those two days weren't agony? They were the worst two days of my life."

"Yeah," I said, lowering my eyes. "She could have had more compassion."

We walked, not ready to be back in the world but not

wanting to be at the clinic, either. Shoals of people swarmed and often parted us, clutching their shopping bags, living their normal lives, not realising the stakes, that we were literally talking about life and, well, not death, we hadn't ever got that far, but not-life.

"It wasn't a walk in the park for me, either," I said, of the last two days.

"It's not the same."

"I didn't say it was the same. *Look.*" I softened my tone and touched her elbow as we waited for the crossing light. On the other side, four people played panpipes. A taxi beeped its horn. A homeless man outside a store selling fancy soap shook a metal tray. It was all so desperately banal.

"Do you think you might need some help, my love?" I said.

"I'm not crazy, okay?" She certainly looked crazy, her eyes bloodshot. "You're looking at me like *they* look at me." The light went green. She darted ahead of me and I had to skip to keep up with her.

"Depressed, I was thinking. Not crazy."

"You don't need to worry about me," she said. "It's you I worry about."

"Me? You're worried about me?"

"Yes. I'm turning up. I'm doing the work. Reading the literature. What are you doing? How are you coping?"

"I'm coping fine."

"Why is your leg shaking?"

"My leg is shaking?" I looked down at my leg, which was shaking.

"Why did you just have to get a mouth guard to sleep?"

"That's normal at our age, no?"

"No," she said. "I'm getting a second opinion. I've had

some contact with a doctor. He's a specialist in this stuff. Co-authored one of those papers." She got her phone out.

I suddenly realised how little I'd known about how Evelyn spent her time at the job she hated but couldn't leave. Turns out she'd been furiously researching, reading, e-mailing, stapling, sticky note-ing.

"You're calling him right now?"

"He's just around the corner."

"He's not going to see us now. This is Germany. Great customer service is when they don't shout at you much."

She called him. He agreed to see us immediately. At least it was all happening quickly. We didn't need any more days like the last two.

A different waiting room. Different chairs, equally emaciated legs. Better plants. I'm not sure how long we sat there because time was being screwy again. Evelyn scrolled on her phone, perhaps hunting down more research, while I wandered around my mind.

"*Adam,*" she said, at some point, with a tone that suggested it wasn't the first time she'd tried to get my attention.

I looked up. "Hmm?"

"Where do you go?"

"What?"

"I said your name three times."

"Oh?"

"Adamistan," she said. "I've never met anyone who lives as much in their own head as you."

I rubbed my jaw. "I wish there were an Adamistan. I bet it would be wonderful."

"I'd like to climb in there," she said, reaching over and tapping the side of my head. "To see it."

"There would be no infertility in it, that's for sure."

"Even better," she said, as they called her name, always

her name, and then we were in a different office, but not really. Swish, minimalist, as if its ribbon-cutting ceremony had ended just five minutes ago. The doctor was a kindly older gentleman, clean-shaven, bald.

Evelyn pushed up her sleeves then lifted the stack of papers from her bag and dropped it onto his shiny empty desk. "I'm not crazy," she said. "I'm informed. Please talk to me accordingly."

He laughed, and I saw respect in the glint of his eyes. He had a nice-grandfather vibe, or the vibe of what I imagined nice grandfathers were like. "I can see how much you want this," he said, flicking through the first six articles. "Oh, there I am." He pulled out his article and held it up. "You're doing everything right, really."

"Do you agree with her?" Evelyn asked, clearly in no mood for platitudes. She'd broadly sketched the situation over the phone.

Her hands were in her lap and she was picking at her fingers. Since when did she pick her fingers? Did I know this new version of Evelyn, this manic version that made scenes and fought out from her corner rather than retreat into it?

"Yes," he said. "Your adenomyosis isn't that bad."

"What do you mean it's not that bad?"

"It's maybe a level 2 out of 4."

"Why has no one ever told me that?"

He drew back his head. "They haven't?"

"All I ever get are clichés about our chances being good and the science getting better every day and not worrying."

"In this field," he said, lifting his hands and twirling them, "you never know why it's not working. You never know why it suddenly works. It's a lot of having to be patient."

I'd never made the connection between the words *patience* and *patient* before.

"I see a lot of couples. Compared to most, you're in a strong position. You could get pregnant naturally, even. It might take three years, but I believe it will happen."

"I don't have three years," she said, quietly.

"So do IVF, but don't downregulate. It's overkill for you two."

We both breathed a long, synchronised sigh of relief.

"I should go back to them?" she asked. "To the clinic?"

"Yes," he said. "They're the best."

I stood and shook his hand and would have happily kissed him on the mouth had he asked.

"Do I need to apologise?" she asked, in his elevator.

"To me?"

"No, not to fucking you, of course. To her. To the doctor."

"*Oh*. Well. Do you think you need to apologise?"

"I don't know. Maybe. I'm going back there to get the meds to start the upcycling. You coming?"

"You need to do that right now?"

"Yes, of course I need to do that right now. Are you coming?"

"Oh, err, well," I said, really wanting to avoid that awkward scene. "It's just I've got my deadline."

"Fine," she said, as we parted at the door. "Like it matters anyway."

18

Late in the afternoon of day four, I was in my room, quietly suffering, when the door opened. It was YoungUriGellar. I assumed he wanted to thank me for ratting out AppleFuckFace and BBQedBill, but all he said was, "You need to go to the meditation hall."

"I'm busy," I said. Did he think these tiles were going to count themselves?

"Goenka has new instructions."

"Hmmm."

Reluctantly I got up, followed him, and took my spot, where I listened as Goenka sang, badly as always. Then he talked, which was when I noticed a difference — Goenka was animated; practically giddy. He congratulated us on making it this far. Assured us the worst was now behind us. That our thoughts would now grow less violent. That we had seen and probably understood our demons. It was time for the next stage, and with it, the full Vipassana experience.

He guided us through some more meditation and then, a change: he extended our area of concentration. We no longer needed to focus on the air as it entered and left the nostrils. We could now focus on it leaving the nostrils and coming into contact with the patch of skin between our nose and upper lip, the central groove, which was called the philtrum, apparently.

Yes, this was our reward for four days of excruciating, backbreaking, enforced nothingness — the philtrum. The first small change in a process that would result in our "observing the entire field of sensations, large and small". He said that if we did this correctly, we would reach a state where all the solidity and rigidity in us would dissolve into a flow of subtle vibrations that would surge through our bodies, and that it would be very pleasant.

That sounded lovely. So lovely, I latched on to this idea and rubbed it like a lotion all over my dry, cracked psyche. Which he seemed to notice because he began a long lecture about how even if it happened — this fizzy energy rush — we mustn't develop any attachment to it. It was as if he were inside my head, hearing my thoughts and, unimpressed by their originality, shooting them down one by one, like low-flying birds. He cautioned that while some people reached this state on day four, others needed eight days, or four courses, or four years.

And then he began another meditation session. Nothing changed for me. A larger sensation area gave me more to focus on, for a few minutes, maybe, before my mind dragged me away to the usual places I didn't want to go.

Two sessions later, Goenka extended the observation area again, widening it to the top of the chin. And not just the breath but all sensations large and small could now be studied.

A session later, he widened it again, to the shoulders.

Ain't it funny how time slips away?

Patiently and persistently, of course.
Another session later, down the left arm.
Then to the left thigh.
Patiently and persistently, again.
Then down to the left knee.
Then back up from the right knee.
Ain't it funny how time slips away?

Then, finally, just before the final session, he let us off the leash. Scan from head to toe, from toe to head. A spring of sensations — usually too small and inconsequential to register in our consciousness — would reveal themselves to us. Could we feel them? We could sweep and they would respond. Not that the point was their response, of course. Not that we should play the game of sensations. We should just observe how much there was to observe, and how none of it was any more important than anything else.

I swept.
I scanned.
There was nothing.
No response.
No sensations.

Which was when Goenka decided that, having given us so much, he'd now need to take something away. We could no longer move during each meditation block, the longest of which was two hours. We were to remain in whatever position we took at the start of each session, no matter the pain, the discomfort, the shouts from our body; we were to be statues. It was only pain, he reminded us. Pain was unimportant. Just a sensation, like all the others. Something that arises to pass away. We should focus on the pain, actually.

What shape did the pain have?
Where did it start and stop?
Pain observed is pain halved, he promised.

He was underestimating how much pain I was in. I now had to hold my back while walking, like some kind of raggedy pensioner. My right knee creaked with each step.

We carried on meditating, and I kept sweeping, to no response. I focused on the pain in my neck and shoulders, but it only grew.

Eventually, the session ended. The lights came on. I opened my eyes. The atmosphere in the room was different. We usually ran out to stretch as soon as the gong sounded. This time, however, everyone just sat there in quiet disbelief. You could feel it in the air, the excitement. It was a sort of intoxicating mist. I looked at my co-meditators. They were dumbfounded.

It had worked. For them. They were racing off to enlightenment while I was going to sit here, broken and embittered, revisiting the worst moments of my life, the only relief being Goenka's singing and telling awful fables about cows and using that tone he used when he said "Western medicine", as if it were dung he'd stood in, barefoot.

I liked Western medicine.

I liked masturbating.

I liked talking.

I liked looking people in the eye.

I liked my past repressed, where it belonged.

I liked sanity.

"Those with questions can come to the front," Grandma Death said.

Half the room got up. They asked and she answered their questions too quietly for me to hear.

I had a question. *Why am I still here? Why am I still torturing myself?*

I stood, flapped my limbs until all the blood returned to them, folded my jumper over my crotch, clutched my lower back with my spare hand, and hobbled out to the forest, where I cried really loudly and punched a tree. At least the pain in my fist distracted me from the pain everywhere else. And it was pain I'd caused. Pain I controlled.

The gong sounded. It was time to go back for more meditation. I tried to walk in that direction, but my feet refused. They turned me, forcing me away from the hall and towards the canteen. First, I'd lost control of my mind. Now, I'd lost control of my feet. They sped off the path and onto the grass towards the small fence.

Beyond that fence were fields.

Beyond the fields, a road.

Follow the road and I'd hit a town called... something.

It was a good time to slip away. To run to town. To call her. It might have worked. Seven eggs. One of them picture-postcard perfect, they had said. Maybe it had worked. Maybe I didn't need to do all this.

"Belgian," I said, remembering that confused doctor and laughing, as I pushed down on the top of the fence.

I glanced around nervously but couldn't see anyone watching. Everybody would be in the meditation hall, at the opposite end of the centre.

I tried to work out if there was a way to break all Goenka's rules at once.

I could go to a restaurant and while masturbating under the table with one hand eat a burger of murdered cow with the other while leaning forward to sip from a straw protruding from a flamboyantly alcoholic cocktail while staring up into the eyes of the waiter, telling him a lie about how much I loved meditation, and then run out without paying.

That would be fun, although maybe less so for the waiter. And then I'd come back here, rejuvenated by sin, ready to do better, to be better.

I climbed the fence. It wasn't high, barely above my hip. More to keep the sheep in the nearby fields out than us in. Sitting on top, as it wobbled beneath me. A whistle. I turned. You know who was there because we've been here before.

"Come down," YoungUriGellar said. "I have bad news."

19

Berlin, Germany, two days before the retreat

It was the room men came to, to come in. Yet they hadn't thought to call it a Masturbatorium. They had several of these rooms in the clinic, and I knew them well. Each was as sad and drab as the next. They had no name. No signage.

In front of me, a sink.

Below me, a glass table with a wireless mouse on it.

Behind me, a reclining vinyl chair covered in paper towels that I wouldn't have sat on for all the bitcoin in Beijing.

To my left, a computer monitor playing a pornographic video called *Lesbian Vampire Academy*. In the fifteen minutes I'd spent watching it, consistently failing to maintain an erection, I'd learned that no one at the academy was a very good vampire. Blood hadn't played a role at all. Nor had crypts, coffins, or crosses. They were also terrible lesbians. Two of them were having very loud, very enthusiastic sex with a man in what I suppose, maybe, if you squinted hard enough, could pass for a classroom. Best I could tell, no one was learning anything.

Meanwhile, I was growing increasingly panicked. Evelyn would arrive soon. We had listened to the doctors. Short protocol. Suppression over, Evelyn's biology now in hyper-drive, today there would be a smash-and-grab on her ovaries. Any fewer than six eggs would be a failure. I wasn't sure how she'd cope with another failure.

But first we needed sperm.

I clicked the mouse to end the video then closed my eyes, tunnelling deep into my memories, channelling happier erotic times with Evelyn. On a holiday in Istanbul, we'd had a joyous, spongy day where everything seemed not only possible, but easy. We'd made love on the couch. Afterwards, we'd eaten ice cream naked and told stories until it was time to make love again. It was one of the better days of my life.

Finished, I put the cup of my seed in front of the little window and rang the bell. I went back to the waiting room. Evelyn was there, sitting on her hands and looking as if she wanted the firing squad to just get it over with already.

"You get the job done?" she asked.

"Just about."

Her pupils bounced around the room. "Nervous."

"I know."

"Will there be eggs?"

I sat down and took her hand. "There will be eggs."

They called her name, and they led us to a room. A new room. I'd thought we'd seen all the rooms. They gave her pills, more pills, but she was always being given pills, and she changed into a hospital gown and we waited for the operating theatre to be free — I guessed, maybe, probably? Or whatever equivalent this place had.

"How many, you think?" she asked.

"At least six," I said. "High quality."

"Six would be good."

We had learned to have modest ambitions.

Two nurses came to collect her.

"Good luck," I said, as if there were something she could influence now. Three cycles, maybe four months, and then it would be over. It would finally be over. I didn't know what over looked like, I didn't know if we could pull Evelyn from the wreckage of all this, but at least it would be over. We would close the project, decide what life after it would entail.

Get a dog.

I was so ready for it to be over.

I tapped some things and then scrolled some things and then remembered I'd never quite got around to installing the baby name app Evelyn had asked me to use months and months ago — actually probably more than a year ago. It would be a nice pick-me-up. I needed to imagine a happy ending. What that happy ending might be called.

I installed the app.

It worked like Tinder: swipe left on a name for no, right for yes. Because my phone and Evelyn's were linked, the app could build a list of those we'd matched on. We no longer talked about names. It was too painful, too presumptuous. But back when we had — in the Istanbul times, the Hasenheide times — we'd noticed that each of us automatically rejected any name the other person suggested, purely because it wasn't our own suggestion.

Spite, I suppose you could call it.

The app was neutral.

In thirty minutes of frantic swiping, I'd worked through over five hundred names. At the end, we'd matched on roughly a dozen girl names but, incredibly, just one boy name: Leo.

The door opened. I rushed to put my phone away, but it wasn't Evelyn. It was a man, tall as a rake. The face he wore was serious, harried, as though he were late for his own autopsy. He was in white trousers and a form-fitting white T-shirt.

"Erm," he said, his forehead etched with worry lines. "So..."

"Keiner Eier?" *No eggs?* My interactions with the clinic had always been in German.

"Seven eggs," he said. "Sufficient. But there's been a complication." His mouth narrowed. "She's now speaking in English? Before we put her under, she was speaking German, but now she only responds in English."

"English?" I said, as if it were an obscure Mongolian herbal supplement. I bit my bottom lip to stop myself from smiling. "But she doesn't speak English."

"Really?" the doctor or doctor-adjacent person said, those worry lines deepening.

"Just German and a bit of Hebrew," I said, fidgeting.

"Hebrew?"

"I know, right?" I rolled my eyes at the ridiculousness of the idea that someone would learn Hebrew before learning English, the world's first second language.

"But are you not..." He hesitated. "Your accent?"

"Belgian," I said. "I'm Belgian."

"Oh." He turned back and said something into the corridor to someone I couldn't see. A minute later the door opened fully. Evelyn entered, pasty like glue, being held up by two nurses. They lowered her stringy body onto the chair next to mine and she smiled sloppily at me, clearly as high as a hundred kites.

"Hello," she said, in English. "I'm back." She blew out an exaggerated breath. "*Woo-hoo*."

"Seven eggs, I hear?" I said, in German.

"More than enough for a good omelette," she replied, in English.

"Unbelievable," the doctor said, in German.

"What?" Evelyn answered, in English. "What is? Should I be worried? Can I get some more of those good drugs? For like the pain or whatever?" Her speech was slurred. "Just saying."

"You're speaking English?" the doctor said, nervously.

She lowered her chin. "Am I? *Oh.* I guess that's my emotional language by now." It was a bit of a weird thing to say, but I blamed the drugs. "He's English," she added, pointing at me but missing and hitting a lowered blind. "Why are they looking at me like that, Adam?"

"No reason, honey," I said, patting her arm. "Just a little joke between the doctor and me."

"Your partner jokes too much," the doctor said to Evelyn, and then left the room, as did the nurses.

Evelyn sat back in her chair and blew the air from her cheeks again. "High as the Himalayas."

"I see that."

"Groggy though." She sat up. "Seven's good. Right? It's good. I think it's good?"

I patted her hand. "It's good. You did good."

It's nearly over.
It's nearly over.
It's nearly over.
What will it mean when it's over?

I know what she thought it would mean. What she'd been hinting at. That I'd have to choose between having a family or having her. That she'd push me to choose the former. But we still had years where, against all the odds, we might accidentally create a lust baby. I didn't want *a* child — I wanted *our* child. And more than that, I wanted her back the way she'd been before.

"Seven," she said again. "It's okay?"

"We only need one. One fresh one. What happens now?"

She went cross-eyed. "Why am I the only one who knows about all the things and the stuff and everything?"

I squinted, and she made a tipping motion with an invisible cup. "Sperm, basically."

"They just tip it on?"

"They tip it on."

"Feels like it's cheating," I said.

"It is cheating. That's the whole point of all this." She wafted her hand around. "It's all cheating. We need to cheat."

"Then they put it in you?"

She made a sucking noise. "If an embryo reaches the blastocyst stage, yes." She blew out another long breath. "I don't think I can do this anymore."

My shoulders dropped. "Me neither."

"But you're not really doing anything."

"Exactly."

"It's not going to work, is it?" Her voice trembled.

"It will work. And if it's a boy, we already know the name," I said, showing her my phone.

She flicked back and forth between the shortlists. "Leo?" she said. "We matched on only one boy name? How is that possible?"

"Turns out I don't like many boy names."

"Me neither. They're all so rraaaaaaaaaaarrr."

"So, Leo?"

"Leo," she said, but then took a sharp breath that became a howl. "Oh god."

"Have the meds worn off already?" I asked at this sudden, unexpected loss of cabin pressure.

"Can you get me more meds?" she pleaded.

"I'll get you your clothes, how about that?"

"I'm down," she said, in her sober voice. "It's over."

I walked to the metal locker behind where she was sitting. "When do you have to come back?" I asked.

"Two days."

"Do I need to be here too?"

"Why would you need to be here?"

"Oh, right."

20

My escape thwarted, I climbed down off the fence. YoungUriGellar waited and then turned around as I reached him, and we walked in step towards the canteen. I felt guilty that I'd planned to leave and hoped that he felt guilty about trying to make me broom.

Would I really have jumped down and run away?

Yes.

A minute later, he held open the door to the accommodation block.

Hang on — I had no phone or money on me. If I had made it to town, what would I have done? I was still not thinking straight, obviously.

We stopped at the door to my room.

"The bad news," he said.

I'd thought my getting caught was the bad news? Why had he waited until now to tell me the bad news? Maybe so no one would see us talking? Was the bad news that they were going to kick me out? Had he led me here to collect my things?

There was no way in hell I was leaving. I had suffered so much and yet learned so little and I would not leave now, empty of insight, heavy with regret. I was fine with leaving if it was what *I* wanted to do. But not if *they* said I had to. No, I would tie myself to that bed. I would kick and scream and bite. They would have to drag me out of this place. It would take an army.

YoungUriGellar abandoned his usual shit-eating grin and lowered his head. "Your grandfather Leo has died," he said. "I'm sorry."

"Ain't it funny how —" I stopped. "S-Sorry?"

"Your grandfather," he said, then gave an obsequious little half bow to excuse himself. He turned and walked down the long corridor and I was alone and very confused, my hand on the door handle, watching him and thinking that he had a very pert bottom, like two apples in a silk sack.

I shook my head. *Focus, Adam.*

Why had he forgotten to punish me for leaving? I hadn't technically left, sure, but intent was nine-tenths of the law, wasn't it? No wait, that was possession. Well, intentions matter, and mine were crappy. I possessed crappy intentions. Maybe he was going easy on me because my grandfather Leo had died? That was nice of him, but also unnecessary, because I didn't have a grandfather Leo. I had a grandfather Ron, who had died long before I was born and had only ever given me one thing — my eyes — and a grandfather Les, who'd died ten years earlier and fortunately had given me nothing because all the things he'd had were corrupted by insanity, what with him being a well-known local madman, nuttier than a wheelbarrow of Ferrero Rocher.

Scratching my stubbly chin, I opened the door and returned to my austere chambers. Freddie was curled in a cramped S, weeping loudly into his chest, as per usual, and I paid him no heed.

I lay down.

That name. Leo. I knew that name, somehow?

Somewhy.

Somewhen.

Ain't it funny how time slips away?

I summoned all my powers of thought and concentration after first checking that there were no new ceiling tiles.

Nope, still twenty-seven.

Time. Slipping. Away.

A memory rose from the deep, like Nessie for a tabloid photographer. The clinic. The eggs. The app. I sat up, my heart racing almost as fast as it had during my panic attack.

DID IT MEAN???!!!

They'd said we wouldn't get any messages from the outside, but there had to be exceptions, surely? Bereavement would be an exception, wouldn't it? Evelyn was fiendishly smart. If she wanted to get a message to me, she would find a loophole.

She had found a loophole. She was communicating, and she was telling me she was pregnant.

Evelyn was pregnant

We were having a child.

Our own child. With our own sperm and our own eggs. A good egg. She would have waited the two days. That meant her HCG levels were doubling. I uppercut the air with joy and leapt out of bed. I did that dance move where you put your hands together and churn butter like an Amish housewife, although they probably don't call them housewives because I think they're all housewives and so there's no real need for that descriptive label.

They're just Amish wives.

I churned butter like an Amish wife. If I hadn't been crying already, as per usual, I would have probably burst into sweet, warm tears of joy. Freddie was crying, although for his own private reasons. I didn't let him drag me down.

Instead, I lay back on the bed and thought about Evelyn and how much I loved her and how excited I was to watch us become parents and how much we had lost in the limbo of wondering whether we ever would be.

I got up.

I paced in a tight circle.

I sat down on the edge of the bed. It was as though there were ants in my pants, which I suppose there could have been. Perhaps an elite unit sent out for revenge after that pathway massacre of four, maybe even five souls.

Do ants have souls?

IVF had worked!

And this pregnancy wouldn't be like the biochemical one with its randomly dispensed, stinky, rotten eggs and lazy, fat, couch-potato sperm that had temporarily fused only to be rejected as nonviable by Evelyn's notoriously picky womb a few days later.

No, this was IVF — a hand-selected, lab-fertilised, artisanal egg, a picture-postcard perfect embryo, they had said, nestling and growing in her pimped-up, science-splashed womb.

We were having a child.

I was going to be a father.

This wretched phase of our lives and relationship was over. I ran out to the meadow and screamed into the faces of daffodils. Gratitude had arisen. I waited to see how long it would last.

It lasted about ninety seconds.

To be honest, I'd hoped for more, but something new arose and shoved gratitude away: terror.

I was going to be a father.

We couldn't mess up parenthood like we'd messed up infertility. Like I was messing up this retreat. I was here, being shown things by my subconscious, but all I was doing was trying to get away from them and back to the breath, just as I'd tried to get away from Evelyn to hide in work or the fun parts of my mind — Adamistan, I suppose.

I had to change my approach. I thought about that for a while and then returned to my room and counted the ceiling tiles and then the gong rang because it was time for the nightly Dhamma Discourse.

21

Popular culture has spread the pernicious lie that we feel one dominant emotion at a time. And that this emotion is, more or less, definable. Which is, of course, as anyone with a pulse can tell you, idiotic. I was going to be a father, and walking to day four's Dhamma Discourse, I was feeling... *everything*.

All of it.

At once.

It rushed in at deafening volume and tremendous speed, a stunning Pollock-splattered shower of emotions.

Excitement.

Fear.

Anxiety.

Hope.

Pride.

Anger.

Jubilation.

I wanted to slow down time (to get more of Evelyn and me, now the infertility stress was over and before we'd have to share our love and her body with a parasite).

I wanted to speed up time (to sooner stare into the eyes of our progeny).

I wanted to read everything ever written about parenting and to ignore it all, to go in as unprepared as possible.

A tiny part of me even hoped we'd lose the baby (maybe because I was afraid we wouldn't raise it right? Or that it might get my family's madness or nose?). I didn't listen to that part. It was stupid.

I wanted and felt many other things, but they were too amorphous to stick labels to.

The doors to the lecture hall opened. I sat down in the centre, back straight. I wasn't expecting much, wasn't even really interested in what Goenka had to say. I had too much thinking and plotting and planning and self-improvement to do.

I was happy to see his wife again. Was she happy? Did she want to be there? Who knew? She never said. Goenka did all the talking. Then he did something unexpected: he got to the fricking point. He set out the core ideology behind Vipassana in such a (mostly) simple manner that I understood it for the first time.

Here is my summary of that summary:

1. The body has six sense doors: eyes, tongue, ears, nose, body, and mind.

2. The body takes in stimuli via these doors and converts them into sensations in the body. Pretty girl walks past, eyes notice this and pass the information inside, where it's converted into arousal, or, if you're sticking with the simplistic saṅkhāra system (craving or aversion), craving, which stirs the loins, a sensation reported in the mind, which thinks things, and perhaps implores you to act, to go talk to the girl, eat the cake, run from the lion, etc.

3. The mind's default pattern is to react to the body's dominant sensations. However, there's no reason to do this. Innumerable biochemical and electromagnetic reactions are occurring constantly throughout it every second. Just as some pre-thoughts become real thoughts that grab your attention, some sensations are deemed important enough to be felt while others — such as a tiny tickle between your fourth and fifth toe or a pulsing in your lower-right earlobe — remain unnoticed.

All of it will pass away.

4. Existence is like sitting in a fast-flowing stream of sensations. Through meditation, you can move to the shore, where you can observe the stream and decide what parts of it you want to bathe in. OBSERVATION, and then ACTION. You don't need to blindly act upon the dominant sensations of the body and thoughts of the mind.

5. In the moments when you are focused on the breath, your mind is free. This impacts the old impurities accumulated in the unconscious. Some of those impurities rise to the conscious level, manifesting as mental or physical discomforts (aches, pains, intrusive thoughts, song lyrics, demons).

6. Observed neutrally, they pass away.

7. Everything passes away.

8. Meditation is not about concentration of the mind, but purification. Go through this purification process often enough and you will move through life with a balanced, equanimous mind less prone to creating impurities in the first place.

The video ended, and for the first time, I wasn't disappointed. I understood some of what I'd been doing wrong here. How wild it had been to even take on this challenge. Despite having no real meditation experience to speak of, I was trying to achieve mastery of my mind. I didn't even have a grasp of the basics. I was reacting to everything, all the time — random mental burps, desires, aversions, ceiling tiles, pre-thoughts, demon loops, Goenka, ants. It was why I was so stompy and shouty and weepy. When my demons arrived, I didn't observe them neutrally. My focus was on getting rid of them, escaping from them, and rushing back to the breath.

If you think you have nothing to learn, it's logical that you stop listening to the teacher. That was what I'd done with Goenka, but also with my mind, which was showing me the same few things for a reason. They weren't passing away, or rather, they were, but only to bounce back immediately because they were trying to teach me something. There was something sitting behind them. They were symptom, not cause.

I vowed that from tomorrow on, I would observe, neutrally, the worst that my mind had to throw, until I found out why it had thrown *that* specific thing.

It was time to hang with my demons.

Yay.

22

Day 5/10: AM
Location: Bed
Mood: Juicy jubilance

The gong vibrated out the morning call to non-prayer. Usually, I'd have been asleep, but today I was awake, sitting across the bed, back to the wall. Freddie was snoring softly. I'd barely slept the previous night; I was going to be a father, and I had so much to think about.

I walked towards the meditation hall. The trees still had dew on their branches. The first few birds were awake, chirping their excitement about another day of... bird activities. I hadn't been up at this unseemly hour since day one, which felt so long ago. I had been a different man then: put together, self-assured, of sound mind. I'm not saying I'd made sense to everyone, but I'd made sense to myself. I no longer made sense to myself — I was a ranting, muttering, raving, horny, gay(ish) loon.

The hall smelt of apples rather than the usual curdled sweat and fresh sorrow. Judging by all the empty places, about 50 percent of my cohorts were either skipping this session or had dropped out, were slinking back into their saṅkhāra-filled lives.

AppleFuckFace's place was empty. Had they kicked him out? If so, I was to blame, and that made me feel both victorious and guilty. Even though he was obviously a hideous person who boiled guinea pigs alive and threw small children down wells, he was also a person and was struggling here, just as I was struggling.

If he'd left, or had been kicked out, I wished him all the worst.

Kneeling on my trusty cushion, I felt a small prick of pride — I'd made it to day five. By lunchtime, I'd be more than halfway through. If Goenka was right, I'd already seen the worst of my mind. I just hadn't watched my thoughts closely or dispassionately.

That was about to change. Eyes closed, I settled in. The session began well, my mind quiet. I was able to observe the breath, patiently and persistently.

In... both nostrils.

Out... both nostrils.

In... left nostril.

Out... right nostril.

I was no longer aroused, which was a great relief. Neither was time and its passing a frequent topic. I stayed with the breath, knowing this would anger my mind and that it would begin its usual process of attempting to distract me by ruining my mental life.

In... both nostrils.

Out... both nostrils.

In... left nostril.

Out... right nostril.

It quickly zeroed in on the topics with which it had best distracted me in the past, plus some new ones related to fatherhood. In particular, a bizarre, high-resolution daydream in which I accidentally cooked our baby instead of a lasagne. The session ground by slowly and, as it did, the distraction queue shrank to just one particular demon. It looped. Again. And again. And again and again again again again again again agianagainagainAGAIN!

I'd watched short snippets of this memory and others of its genre many hundreds, or perhaps even thousands of times over the last three days. Never willingly, though. I'd just endure a few seconds of it before shaking it away or shouting over it.

This time I watched closely. I pretended to be enraptured. An enthusiastic front-row audience member. "Encore," I shouted inside, each time it ended. "Encore!" The more I watched it — the more I gave myself to it, the more I put myself in the body of the eleven-year-old me starring in it — the more vivid it became, the less aware I was of thirty-six-year-old me until...

Something very strange happened. The sensation was like that of being grabbed at the crown of my head and pulled sharply backwards, as if I were a rubber band. Taut, it was released, and with a *thhhhwwwwuppp* sound I shot down, swirling and turning through the many layers of my mind.

I felt my eyes open, but I wasn't controlling them. I was in a... classroom, looking at a dusty blackboard, sitting behind a small wooden desk. I tried to look down to see what I'd been writing, what I was gripping, but no matter how hard I concentrated, I couldn't move my body — my eleven-year-old body. The body I was locked inside of. I could feel what this younger Adam was feeling — a mixture of hunger and fear — but I had no control over him. I was simply sitting, staring out through his eyes, unable to decide when they blinked or upon what they should gaze.

He turned his head, this Adam. It was a mobile classroom. Middle school. Light streaming in through windows smeared with handprints. He then looked down at the desk and I could see it was a green pencil I was gripping, a pencil that needed sharpening. He appeared to be colouring a map of the Americas. He'd not stayed within the lines. A shout came from outside. He looked left. Along the wall were pull-out trays. His was at the very bottom, the handwriting admirably poor, as if he'd wielded the pen drunk on fruit juice. He hadn't crossed the *t* of Fletcher.

Something crossed my vision from the right. A paper plane. "Who threw that?" the teacher asked with mock annoyance. He bent down to pick it up after it dived sharply and landed near his desk, its nose bent beyond repair.

"Middle school," a familiar voice said, and the scene skidded to a stop. Everything froze and the colours bleached away, leaving only shades of grey. A low-fidelity, full-colour Evelyn appeared in front of me, crackling into view as if between channels on an old television. She flapped her arms. "I think I'm some sort of ghost?" she said. "How naff."

"What are you doing here?" I asked, somehow, despite being unable to move my mouth. She was wearing the same outfit as the last time I'd seen her, in the living room, before I'd left for the retreat: blue knitted jumper, comfortable blue jeans. Even had her fluffy white slippers on. Only the tea was missing.

"I can't even move," I said. "I'd love to be a ghost."

Her head tilted. "Wait. Say something else?"

"Are you really pregnant?" I asked.

"You're right," she said. "Your lips don't move when you talk." She looked around. "This is a memory, right? You can't move because you can't change it, I guess? My god, your glasses."

I was wearing the oversized gold-rimmed glasses I'd stubbornly refused to change until I was sixteen, roughly ten years after fashion had bored with ridiculing them. They were bent to the point of parody. It looked like I was wearing them for a bet. No wonder this memory looked so smeared and grimy.

"How come you're here?" I asked. "You were never here before. And I've seen this memory a lot. Too much. Well, I was never in it, not like I am now. I'm confused. Are you confused? I'm rambling. These days, I'm always confused. I'm mentally ill now, by the way. So, thanks for that."

She tried to touch me but her hand passed straight through. "I'm not actually here, obviously. I'm you being me." She smiled widely and didn't seem disturbed by any of this — more amused, as if this were all a funny lark; a nice way to fill the day. "It's all a bit of a rip-off of *The Christmas Carol*, isn't it?"

"Are you saying my imagination isn't very imaginative?"

She angled her head, grinning down at me. "Look at your hair." It was thick and shiny. I'd forgotten that I'd ever had thick and shiny hair. Any head hair, really. Mum used to blow-dry it each morning. Evelyn reached over to tussle it, forgetting there was no point. Her ghost hands disappeared into it.

"It was the jewel in my genetic crown," I said, and then regretted it, because I mean, really, what kind of sentence was that? And I was supposed to be eleven. "The ghosts led the tour in *A Christmas Carol* though, right? You're not leading here. It ended when you talked. Talking of talking, we have a lot to talk about when I get out of this place. I have a lot to apologise for. I didn't help you with your demons, but I knew you would help me with mine, and now here you are. Which is nice. However grainy. I talked to a worm the other day, and it talked back."

"Jesus, you are rambly." She was looking out at the playground, which was half covered in mobile classrooms. The grass was patchy and the basketball rings had no nets. "You conjured me here to help you?" she asked, bending to look at fish swimming in a tank beneath the window.

"Yes."

A bell sounded. She looked up. "What was that?"

"Maybe that was the end of the meditation session?" I guessed. "No, can't be two hours." Nothing happened when I tried to open my eyes. I swallowed my irritation down. I was passive. Stuck. At the mercy of whatever this was. "I think we're stuck here until we figure out why this demon memory keeps looping."

Another ding.

She froze. "Odd," she said.

"Maybe by channelling you, I'll get more distance from the memory? You're kind of like a neutral observer, maybe?"

DING

"The dings are annoying," she said.

"The dings are me, aren't they" I said, having noticed they only rang in response to statements I made.

DING

"It's when I get the right answers," I said. "The dinging."

DING

Her nose scrunched, which I interpreted as her finding that lame. "Where do they come from, though? How do we know we can trust them?"

I considered it. "Goenka talks about the layers of the mind. How you can know things on different levels. How you can *feel* something is wrong in your stomach, no matter how much your higher, more rational mind is arguing for it. I think the bell is coming from lower in my subconscious."

DING

"You're not worried that the worm talked back?" I asked, remembering she hadn't even commented on that particularly startling revelation.

She lifted her chin. "The worm didn't talk back. You talked for it. Just as I'm not me — I'm you being me."

"You're being very matter-of-fact."

She nodded. "Facts matter."

"Well, even as an out-of-focus ghost, I think you're a pretty convincing you. Are you really pregnant?"

"Yes," she said.

"That's exciting."

"You don't sound excited."

"I can't move my mouth, or my... anything at all. But I didn't sleep at all last night and I'm terrified, but it's nice that you're here. That I'm not alone with all this."

She looked around giving lots of small nods, like a plumber assessing a job. "Middle school shouldn't be too complicated," she said. "Let's get you fixed so we can celebrate that pregnancy and be terrified but excited together when you've done your ten days."

"Okay," I said. "Good. Yes. Let's do it."

"Why is this a trailer?" she asked, turning towards the blackboard. Like many Germans, she'd learned much of her English from American TV shows and often defaulted to American English. "We never had classes in trailers in my school."

"We're poor," I said. "The school is over capacity. Each year, they add another one or two of these mobile classrooms. It's very, very hot." I was in my navy-blue polo top. It bore the logo of the school: a white ship. "Does Ghost You feel the heat?" I asked.

"No," she said. "What happens now? How do we get it to play, the memory?"

"I think we have to be quiet," I said.

DING

23

Evelyn crackled out of view as colour flooded in from the edges of my vision like water into a washing machine's drum.

"Slowly," the teacher said, tapping on the blackboard. "And don't forget your homework. Pages 22 and 23. TOMORROW. That's the day after today."

The class was already on its feet and in disarray, loose sheets and workbooks stuffed carelessly into folders. Folders disappearing into bags. Kids shoving and shouting and rushing for the door.

Unable to talk or move while the memory played, I just sat there, watching, reminding myself that that's what I was here to do.

Young Adam didn't move, but I felt his heartbeat speed up.

The teacher packed his briefcase. Why did a middle school teacher need a briefcase? For his banana? I tried to remember his name. Was it a colour? I settled on Mr White. He readjusted his dark-blue tie, which was covered in garish bright flowers. He was enormous, well over two metres, and had a narrow skyscraper face.

He took a last sip of what must have been cold coffee out of a mug that said *World's Greatest Teacher*. He dropped the mug hard on his desk and marched down the aisle towards the door, not noticing I was still in my seat, looking nervously left and right.

There was only one other boy left. He walked over to me. "You coming, Adam?"

It was my friend Tim. A thin boy with skin the colour of gruel whose nose permanently leaked like a broken tap. He was the sort of child other women gave their children's snacks to. He lacked an understanding of social nuances and shunned eye contact. Our friendship was held together by a mutual love of Super Nintendo and his very large back garden. My parents had four jobs each while his parents didn't seem to work or have any discernible income.

"I'll catch you up," I heard my younger self say. A lie. "Need to sort my bag out."

I (technically *he*, but since I was in his body, feeling what he felt and it had once happened to me, I'm going to stick with *I* from here on out) slipped off my chair and headed towards the large walk-in cupboard at the back of the classroom, behind the blackboard.

I opened the door, slid some plastic bags full of workbooks to the side and created a little nook to hide in under some painting aprons and a white lab coat hanging on the pegs. I positioned them in front of me and pulled my legs up to my chest, my arms hugging them tightly.

Evelyn reappeared in front of me. Half her body was in the cupboard, half was floating through the door and into the classroom.

"Whatcha doing?" she asked breezily.

"Chilling," I said.

Her eyes widened. "In a cupboard, behind some coats?"

"Best place to chill, init?"

"You're hiding."

I looked around as if surprised. "Hiding? Here? How dare you."

"Uh-huh," she said. "Fine. So, this is just a pivotal memory of you chilling in a cupboard, is it?"

"Yeah, it's one of my top-five greatest chills. In about ten minutes I get so relaxed I fall asleep and miss music class. It's epic."

"Hmm," she said. "As much as this banter is enjoyable, we both know something big is about to go down and so we might as well take it seriously, no?"

"Speak for yourself."

"Who are you hiding from?" she asked. "Just tell me that."

I shrugged a shoulder. "No one."

"Bigger kids?"

"Maybe."

"I'm sorry."

"It's cool." It wasn't cool, and inside I was cuddling a cactus. "Where are you when the memory is playing?" I asked, to change the subject.

"I'm there," she said. "You just can't see me anymore. Why are they after you, the bigger kids?"

"They're jealous of my mum-blow-dried hair and stylish gold"—I reached up to my nose—"very mangled glasses."

She pushed out her lips but said nothing.

"I don't think there's a reason. I mean, one of them will say I looked at him funny or something. But there's no reason, really. Why did you interrupt, anyway? Shall we not just get this over with?"

"I wanted a bit more context," she said. "To prepare myself."

"Very German."

"Thanks. How long is the lunch break?"

"Like forty-five minutes?"

"You're going to hide in here for forty-five minutes?"

"Nah, my best friend, that kid, Tim, he's already told them where I am."

Her eyes narrowed. "Why would he tell them?"

"Kids are dicks, basically."

"He was very snotty," she said. "And that's not a judgement, just an observation. Like, his nose was running."

"He's always like that."

Satisfied with the context, she straightened, closed her eyes, and dissolved into snow.

The memory continued.

My hands, resting on my knees, shook. A few minutes passed before the classroom door creaked open.

"He didn't come out," I heard Tim say.

"The cupboard," another voice said excitedly. "What a wimp."

"Loooooser," said someone else.

"Let's get him."

"Come out, come out, wherever you are," another sang.

"We won't hurt you," another said, and they all snickered.

The bottom half of my body was shaking uncontrollably. The door to the cupboard flew open. I had forgotten to hold it closed. The snickering became laughter. They had exposed me hiding shamefully in a nook of my own creation.

"I was just looking for you," I said, trying humour on the main bully, a redheaded kid with freckles and braces. Redheads in this school had only two choices: retreat or attack. He'd picked the latter. He was in the year above, the top year, where puberty had found him early. He already had a thin wisp of ginger hair on his top lip. His arms and hands were longer and stronger than they should have been.

He was gangly and confused and straddling a quickly widening gap between childhood and early adolescence.

And that hair.

I mean.

His mother also styled his but didn't preen over it, as mine did. No, his mother occasionally dropped a bowl on his head and trimmed around it. Not even straight; the fringe hung lower on the left-hand side. He had several older brothers who were also renowned in the town and one of which would go to prison for assault with a deadly weapon. I've either forgotten or suppressed the bully's name, so I'll just call him Freckles.

Freckles laughed and turned to the others. "What a twat."

He pulled me out by my feet.

"Get off."

"Grab him."

"No!" I shouted. "Stop."

There were five kids, plus Tim, who was just standing there rubbernecking, his face as inexpressive as usual, neither encouraging nor condoning. Freckles and his friends dragged me along the ground until my head smacked into a table leg.

"Aaahh," I yelled. "I didn't do anything. Get off."

"You looked at me funny," Freckles said.

"I didn't. *Help*," I shouted, as Freckles booted me in the groin and another kicked me in the back of my head.

"Help me drag him."

"I'm sorry," Evelyn said, reappearing to swipe furiously at the gang, her arms going straight through. "I can't help. There's nothing I can do."

"It's better if you don't watch," I said.

"This is nothing to be embarrassed about," she said. "You're not at fault here."

"I was kind of weird."

"You're like, what, ten? All ten-year-olds are weird."

"Don't watch," I said. "Please?"

"I'm watching. We'll go through this together and then we'll figure it out."

Shame grows in the dark. An Evelyn expression, although it was probably from something she'd read. She was always reading. Not that this was shameful. It was just kid stuff. And anyway, she was also me, even if it didn't feel like it.

I scrabbled to my knees and was half-crawling away when they dragged me outside by my collar. There were three metal steps to get down from the classroom, sharp and heavy.

"I'll walk down," I said. "Let me go."

They did, but as soon as my feet hit the ground, I took off running. I was fast when I was young and, on this day, I had a reason to be; chest inflated, head back, arms pumping, I created a gap between me and the kids chasing me. I looped around two mobile classrooms and emerged onto the main field, but the chase was attracting attention. It had already stopped a nearby football game, a basketball match, and a dozen people playing something called British Bulldog, which would get banned in a few weeks after Tim ended up in hospital with a neck injury.

"Get him," Freckles yelled.

"Stop Four Eyes" said another, waving his arms at a group of children playing marbles ahead of me by the chain-link fence. Three girls who were skipping abandoned their rope and ran for me. As did a few British Bulldog players. And a marbler. I was running out of field and places to loop to avoid all the people now chasing me. Running along the fence, I swerved from several outstretched hands until I was in a small clearing between bushy conifer trees in the corner of the playground. I circled a tree, jigging and shimmying, and wriggled free from a boy who had grabbed my top, which ripped at the collar. For a moment, I felt as if I might get away, even though I knew I didn't.

Directly ahead was the edge of the paved football pitch. All the players had stopped to watch.

"Get him!" Freckles yelled again, waving his arms and miming punching. "Or I'll get you!"

Several of the players ran at me.

"Dickhead."

"Grab him."

"Come on!"

It was incredible how fit I was at this age. Even after this long run, I was barely out of breath. But now kids were coming from all directions and there was no safe place to run. A chant started up, quiet at first but growing with each repetition. "Fight, fight, fight, FIGHT."

This chant was a siren call, irresistible. It rallied children faster than "Fire", "Chocolate", "Home time", "Summer holidays", and "Next goal wins".

"No!" I shouted, flailing my arms, slowing down. "No fight. There's no fight."

Suddenly, the entire school rushed over. I was stuck. Gave up. Stopped. Held up my hands. Dropped to my knees on the scrubby grass as kids grabbed me from all sides. I let out a fake nervous laugh as the first kid punched me in the stomach. I crumpled over as Freckles kneed me in the face, finally breaking my glasses.

Standing by the fence, maybe fifteen metres away, were two dinner ladies watching on, doing nothing.

Blood from my nose.

"Bundle" was the new shout. "Bundle, bundle, BUNDLE!" A dozen boys jumped on top of me and my chest collapsed and I started to cough and splutter. I tried to crawl out between legs, but I was stuck firm under a mass of bodies.

I thrashed frantically, trying to get away, but too many bodies held me down. Freckles took a run-up and launched himself onto the top of the bundle, which collapsed under his weight. He was laughing manically and contorted himself to try to reach me. I stopped writhing. There was no point.

"Make him eat this," said Ryan, a boy I sat next to in English, someone else I'd thought of as a friend. He was holding up a worm. It was wiggling, trying to get free. In that regard, we had a lot in common.

"I need to stop this," Evelyn said, and the action froze and the lights dimmed. I looked up at her, my head hanging out of the bundle, the rest of me stuck firm.

"Don't," I said. "Let's get this over with."

"I can't watch it."

"Why *are* you watching it?"

"I thought I wanted to, but I can't. But I have to, it seems. And I'm just so sorry." Her face was full of compassion.

"It's okay," I said, sucking in air. "Just, you know, school stuff. High school is worse."

She looked around the playground. "This is nothing like *my* school."

"It's just generic bullying. Tomorrow it will be someone else."

"Is that true?"

"Probably."

"Well, you're not alone," she said, and straightened. "I am here. Just, you know, not in any useful capacity."

I sighed because I obviously was alone and by talking to me, she was making the memory last longer than it had to.

No, wait, I reminded myself. The goal was not to rush

out of this. I needed to live it. To feel every emotion I'd felt. To watch and to learn, without judgement.

"Thank you," I said.

She lowered her head. My past played once more. I refused to open my mouth as someone punched me repeatedly in the kidneys and Freckles, who was on my back, took my arm and twisted it behind me and prised it upwards.

"Open your mouth or I'll break your arm."

The pain was a red-hot poker to the throat. I was just about holding myself together. Crying was a big deal here, for a reason that made about as much sense as anything else that happened here.

Mr White walked over, a new cup of coffee in his hands. "What's going on here?"

"Help," I said.

"It's his birthday," Freckles said, ruffling my excellent hair. There was a weird tradition in this school, maybe in all English schools — hazing was allowed if it was the person's birthday.

"It's not my birthday," I said, or tried to, because the bully slipped his hand over my mouth and nose. It smelt of cigarettes. The kids turned to the teacher, awaiting judgement.

"Hurry up," the teacher said, and turned away. Authority figures. To this day, I have a real problem with authority figures. That's why I'd reacted so strongly to Evelyn saying the opposite.

"Eat it, eat it, eat it!" was the new chant.

I didn't want to, but I wanted this to be over and really, how much worse could it get? How much more embarrassing?

Slowly, I opened my mouth. Ryan pushed in the worm and then lifted his arms as if he'd scored an important last-minute penalty.

The crowd groaned with disgust.

Shouting.

Boos.

I chewed. The worm tasted like nothing, with a hint of sour dirt. It wasn't necessarily an unpleasant taste. Freckles let go of my arm but stayed sitting on me. I spat out the worm, now in two. The bodies around me did their own wriggling, trying to extricate themselves. The dinner ladies stared on, faces blank, as if we were just dogs fighting over a tennis ball.

The wave of emotion finally broke, and I began to wail and sob, pushing my head down into the dirt as if trying to hide.

That did it. The mob recoiled. There were boos as the bell rang to signal the end of the break. The children scattered — grabbing their marbles, water bottles, skipping ropes, navy jumpers — and returned to class. I lay on the ground, crying, looking up into the conifer tree's thick branches.

The sky above was blue. Cloudless.

My charcoal-coloured trousers were ripped and so was my polo top. Both my shoes were gone. Someone had thrown them high into one of the trees.

Evelyn returned.

"I was just about to take them," I said jovially.

"Who?"

"Err... all of them? I was lulling them into a false sense of security."

She frowned. "They definitely seemed secure."

"I didn't have to eat the worm either. I was just curious, you know? And I thought it would be a good story to tell later."

"Weird that you never told me about it then, right?"

"Just shows how inconsequential I found it."

"Hmm," she said. "That's kind of confusing."

The scene had ended with me looking towards the trees. "I remember now that Tim's older brother told us there was a secret base in these trees. We searched for it for years."

She looked at the small space. "You searched around these two trees for years?"

"We weren't very methodical."

She sat down, put her ghost hand over mine. "Many cultures eat worms," she said. "The Māoris, for one. And a few in India. We'll probably all eat them in the future."

"I was a hipster even then," I said, as the realisation that this was all over, that I wasn't this Adam anymore, that I'd never have to be him again, soothed me.

"I'm sorry," she said again.

I blew a raspberry. "Why? It's fine. Just the usual rough and tumble of young minds and bodies clashing in a poorly supervised setting."

"This was not normal."

"Yeah, it was."

Her tone hardened. "It was not okay. Stop minimising."

"If this is a significant memory, I'm embarrassed."

DING

"Ah, the dings are back," I said. "I almost forgot about them."

"Of course this is a significant memory. Pretty much the whole school beat you up and made you eat a worm."

"Oh, come on. It was half the school, at most. And it was just a little worm. And anyway, so many people's childhoods are like this. It's a cliché, almost. And this was not the worst day of my school life."

No ding, I noticed.

"So why are we back here, then?" she asked. "If what you're saying is true. Is it important because it's where you caught a terrifying, debilitating fear of worms you've never told me about?"

"No," I said, but then remembered Hasenheide, the worm she'd found. "Well, probably not."

"Of course it matters," she said, looking up at the trees. "How could this not matter?"

"Everyone's bullied," I said. "This is just your classic, garden-variety, small-town cruelty."

Again, no ding.

"You noticing the lack of dings?" she asked. "Because I am."

"Fuck the dings," I said.

"You've changed your tune on the dings."

"It's disconcerting to realise how little you can trust your own reading of things, you know?"

She nodded.

"There's just nothing particularly special about this. I don't want to include it in the stories I'll tell of my Vipassana experience. Especially if it becomes a book one day, like everything in my life. Most memoirists have serious issues they're grappling with, you know? They're born into cults. Or have crazy stepparents who think God sends them messages through poop, like Augusten Burroughs. Or they overcome great odds, or at least climb great mountains. I'm just a tediously ordinary, privileged middle-class white man. My parents loved me. Fiercely. They never once found a message in their poop."

DING

Evelyn folded her arms. "The people who read your books do so *because* they're like you. You're the everyman. That's your whole shtick. They're grappling with the same questions, issues, insecurities, boredom, shame, inadequacy. We all are."

"Maybe," I said, which was often what I said in the face of inconvenient truths. "Maybe."

"And anyway," she continued, "life is relative. You aren't twice as happy as a man with half your number of legs. It's just not how it works."

I took a deep breath. "So how does it work, then, since you have all the answers, apparently?"

She threw up her hand and let it drop. "It's about how you feel about yourself, of course."

Evelyn had a very interesting mind in that she loved living but hated herself most of the time. She had no problem giving a presentation in front of a hundred strangers but would come very close to throwing herself in front of a train if she had to make two minutes of small talk with a stranger on a train-station platform. She was full of ripe, juicy contradictions. I thought of Freddie.

"If this is here, if we're here, this was a pivotal moment," she said. "Even if that's inconvenient for you to admit."

"It would be easier to take you seriously as my ghost therapist if you weren't wearing fluffy white slippers."

She looked down. "If I could take them off and beat you with them, know that I would. And you're deflecting again."

"They're fluffy."

"Wouldn't matter. But stop making jokes. Focus on why we're here."

"Well," I said, not because I had anything with which to follow that *well*, but because I wanted to start confidently. The *well* was bait I threw out into the conversation's pond hoping something more substantial would nibble on it.

Nothing happened. No nibbles.

"What were you feeling when it was happening?" she asked, after a minute of silence.

"Well," I said again, "actually, during the bundle, when I was being repeatedly pummelled and air was a luxury good, a curious thing happened. It was like I was pulled up out of my body and into my head. Once there, I felt nothing. I was just sort of floating. I forgot about it until now, until reliving it here."

DING

"Sounds like you disassociated," she said.

"I, well, I don't know if it was that extreme, but it felt..." I paused to find a word. "Significant?"

DING

"I wish I could go back and tell this little guy that it gets better, you know?" I said. "That he gets to date women like you and..." I hesitated. "Well, really just one woman like you, but that's plenty."

"Sweet," she said, blowing me a ghost kiss.

"Kids are mean and teenagers are the worst, but being an adult is great. He will escape. Get control."

DING

"Control," I said. "*Huh.*"

"You're a mega control freak," she said. "You hate surprises and don't even like it when I buy you presents because you're" — she lowered her voice — "obliged to be happy about them."

"You don't buy me presents."

"Why do you think that is? Why don't *you* buy *me* presents?"

"Why would I force you into the same obligation bind?"

"You're full of shit."

"And worm, apparently."

The half-chewed worm lay near my sock. At least it hadn't talked to me, begged me not to eat it. I suddenly remembered something. "Around this time, I started getting out of bed and sleeping on my bedroom floor, blocking the door."

"Why?"

"My parents assumed it was an eccentricity. I don't remember doing it, just that they told me I did it. I think it was about control. My room didn't have a lock."

She squinted. "Was anyone coming in?"

"No," I said, and laughed. "My home life was wonderful. Was nothing like this place."

It went silent and, for a moment, I almost expected the scene to resume or loop back to the beginning. Which, fortunately, it didn't. "I always felt too sensitive when I was young."

DING

"Interesting," she said, her head tipping back. "Would Adult Adam say that about himself, do you think?"

I laughed. "No. Well, all life is suffering," I said. "The Buddha was right. Hey, wait. Maybe that's the link to us? To our problems?"

"The Buddha?"

"No. Control. How when you don't have it, you suffer. It's like you in the clinic with all those highlighted journal articles. That was you taking control."

"I don't see the link."

"I feel like I made a rule after this experience: if I'm in control, I'm safe. And that's not a bad rule, has probably served me well, even if it means I hate surprises and presents. But it must also make relationships difficult, right? Because being in a meaningful relationship requires you to give up control to someone," I said. "Which is scary."

If I could have clapped, I'd have clapped. "And the Baby Project was the same," I continued. "There, we had to give control to the fertility clinic. And they weren't motivated to take our feelings into account. And I was like a substitute warming up on the sidelines waiting to be called into the game, but they never called me, because I'm just the sperm. I'm useless. That's maybe why this memory is here now, during this retreat. It connects to infertility. To us. It's control. That's what's behind this demon — not self-hatred, inadequacy, shame, fear, self-loathing."

"Wait," she said, as a single, wasn't-that-obvious *DING* was followed by a longer, booming *GONG*.

The scene faded. My eyes, my real eyes, opened: I was on my back in the meditation hall. Bodies were shuffling towards the exit. I could hear at least three people crying. I stared up at the ceiling (hundreds of tiles) as one of the dozen giant fans whirred above me.

I was back. I pumped my hands and twirled my feet. I had control again. I was no longer locked in. My mind felt refreshed; minty, almost. I had stopped looking away and was making progress at long last.

Evelyn had been right to send me here. I wasn't completely mined. Didn't know myself as well as I'd thought. Didn't understand how the experiences in my past had become behaviours I no longer wanted in my present.

I sat up, closed my eyes, and returned to the breath.

In... left nostril.

Out... left nostril.

In... both nostrils.

Out... both nostrils.

In... right nostril.

Out... right nostril.

In... left nostril.

Out... both nostrils.

I'm not sure how long I stayed like that, but at some point, the meditators returned for the next session and I was still with the breath. I joined Goenka on the next full-body sweep, which was what our sessions were about now, occasionally guided, mostly alone.

"Sweep, from the very top of the head to the ends of the toes," he said.

I concentrated with all my mental strength on the top of my head, but no sensation responded. I went back to the breath for a while. Then I tried to wander from the ends of my nostrils down my philtrum to the top of my lip, but there was no reply.

I opened my eyes and punched my floor cushion. Even if I was making progress, it wasn't enough. I went to bed annoyed, but that was nothing new.

24

Day 6/10: AM
Location: Bed
Mood: Exquisite confusion

I got up with the 4am gong and trudged to the meditation hall weary but knowing I had to get to work. I had made progress the previous day, but it was hard-won. I had the first piece of a puzzle but didn't know how many pieces there were, or what the image I needed to assemble looked like. I had four more distraction-free days to find out. I took my spot, picked my position, and narrowed the focus of my attention.

In... right nostril.
Out... right nostril.
In.... both nostrils.
Out... both nostrils.

The queue formed. The thoughts were familiar, the topics painful. The worm turned up once or twice more, but eventually, there was just one major demon looping. I watched it with rapt attention, focusing on putting myself into the body of the me in it, an early-twenties Adam this time, his thinning, receding hair spiky and gelled. The more I watched, the more I saw, the more porous the boundary between him and me felt and then there was that stretching sensation and the snapping sound as I was fired down into the past.

Thhhhwwwwuppp.

A train. The lights cut in as we left a tunnel and rushed towards the next station. The dumbphone in my pocket vibrated. I — rather, this younger me that I'll call *I* again — pulled it out. There was a message from my girlfriend at the time, Sarah.

> Sarah: There's something I need to tell you. Make sure I do, even if I don't want to. Okay?

I slid it back into the pocket of my egregiously baggy denim jeans.

"Look at your hair," a voice said, and the memory stopped and the lights, already low, dimmed. "It's magnificent."

Evelyn was sitting in the seat next to mine.

"Hi," I said. "Does it make you kind of seasick? The journey here?"

"No. I just appear."

"I'm happy you're here," I said, because she had done most of the work last time, in that matter-of-fact, no-nonsense way of hers.

She inspected the carriage. "London, right?"

"Yeah. We just left Liverpool Street."

"You were so skinny," she said with a laugh. "What were you eating back then?"

"Sherbet, mostly."

"You kind of remind me of someone," she said, tapping the end of her nose. "Who is it?"

"Ross from *Friends*. I got that a lot."

"Please tell me you're not about to get beaten up again?" she asked. "I can't watch that a second time."

"Nah," I said. "This one's not bad either. Barely anything, really. I've told you about it," I said, but remembered I hadn't, not really. I'd told her a sanitised version of it with all the embarrassing, lumpy bits strained out.

"BEING PUBLICLY HUMILIATED AND MADE TO EAT A WORM IS BAD," she said. "Okay? Just accept it."

"Right, yeah. *Fine*. Well, this one is more weird than shameful. I'm actually really surprised it's here. I always thought it was a positive experience."

"Okay," she said, settling herself back. "I don't believe you, because you lie to yourself all the time. But anyway. Let's do it. I'm ready."

Sound rushed back in. The train rattled on the tracks. The lights above us flickered on and off. Three stations later, at King's Cross, I got off. My steps were fast in my canvas trainers as I wound my way up a maze of escalators and stairs past sad, shrivelled commuters. A smell of distrust hung in the air, amplified by the lenses of CCTV cameras that watched from every corner.

I emerged, as if from a monster's mouth, into a street clogged by a rubbish lorry that smelt of death and gravy and was emptying the bins of a seedy nightclub into its belly to the sound of glass bottles breaking. I checked my watch; a Swatch. I'd had a collection of them, I now remembered. Was sure they'd be valuable one day. Was sure I'd be rich. A millionaire by thirty, I always said to people. I don't understand now why I'd thought much of what I'd thought at this age, but I appreciated the conviction with which I'd believed it. I was going to set the world alight and then dance around its flame. All lips would speak my name, if only once. I would get my own street, no, a building shaped like my face, no, my own cult, no, my own city — Adamistan.

I walked down a busy high street past the overpriced deli that was Sarah's favourite. In it, every item came with a thick, embossed card containing an elaborate story about how the pig would have begged to be slaughtered had it known just how tasty its insides were going to become.

I started running. Went around a corner. Darted across a road a few seconds after a green crossing light turned red. An annoyed cab driver beeped me. There was a school and the sound of children playing. Nicely, even, from what I could hear. A swaggering teenager barged into me with his shoulder and didn't apologise. I pretended not to notice. I pulled on a door. A restaurant. Spanish themed and with a bull as its logo. I'd been here a few times with her. We liked the sangria. It came in brown terra-cotta jugs.

Sarah was inside, at a table in the middle of the half-full restaurant. She sat in the seat that faced the door. Many of the dark tables were covered in dirty glasses and plates, uncleared from the end of the lunchtime rush. She looked up from a business book about someone moving someone's cheese. Her career in finance was starting well.

She didn't smile when she saw me, just gently lowered and closed the book, her lips pressed tightly together. She had pale skin, thin, shoulder-length black hair, and wore a lot of green. Today it was a green blazer over a crisp white shirt. She had a small nose; I'd always liked that about her. She sang in the shower. Couldn't be in a room with alcohol without making its acquaintance. For months, she hadn't opened her mail. She made the sign of the cross every time she handed her bank card over. We'd been together for two years and I loved her the most out of any woman I had ever met.

"Sorry," I said, leaning over the corner of the table to hug her. "Trains were a nightmare, as usual. Leaves on the track? What kind of a nonsense —"

She neither got up nor returned the hug, just sat stiff as a pole and interrupted me. "You won't want to hug me when you know what I've done."

"I'm sure I will," I replied, yanking back a chair and sitting down opposite her.

She pulled a tissue from her bag. She never carried tissues in her bag. Wasn't that kind of girl. Didn't think ahead. Wasn't prone to emotional outbursts. She blew her nose. "I'm sorry," she said.

"What's going on?" I asked, looking around for the waiter. "Your mum's operation go okay?"

The waiter arrived. "Top of the..." He looked down at his watch. "Early afternoon." He doffed an invisible hat. "Sorry, I mean *Hola*. I used to work in an Irish bar." He flashed a smile, had nice teeth. "I'm new, but you won't notice." He had a silver earring and scruffy hair dyed blue. He was bouncing on his tiptoes. Thespian, I decided. "Are we well today?" he asked. "Sure we are."

We each gave him one of those wide-but-impossibly-shallow British smiles required fifty times a day — the kind that tires your soul like a ten-kilometre run. "Good," said the amateur thespian, as he passed a menu to Sarah and then one to me. "I'm Steven. If you want to hear any of the specials, let me know. *Gracias*."

I rolled my eyes. Steven slipped away. Sarah bit her lip.

"Sarah," I said. "What's —"

"I cheated on you," she blurted. "At that team off-site."

I dropped the menu, which hit the corner of the table and tumbled to the floor. I left it there. "What?"

"I'm sorry," Sarah mumbled.

"What?" I said again, eventually, as if I'd simply misheard.

"I didn't. It just..." Her eyes filled with tears.

"Who." I picked up the menu. "*With?*"

She shook her head. "No one."

"How could it be no one?" I said. My voice reached for and found anger. "It wasn't a ghost, was it?"

Evelyn laughed; the scene stopped.

"Don't laugh, please."

She cleared her ghost throat. Straightened. "Sorry. It's just—"

"Ghost, yeah, I get it."

The waiter returned, clapped his hands. "How you two getting on there, amigos? Can I take your drink orders? *Lovely.*"

"I," she said. "I. *Erm.*" She looked from him to me. "Are you staying?"

"Eh?" I scowled. "Why wouldn't I —"

"Wine," she said. "Large one. No. *Bottle.*"

"Would you like a recommendation?" he asked. "White or red?"

"Yes. *No.* I mean, just get what you were about to recommend. *Red.*"

"Rolling the dice," he said, making guns with his fingers. "Love it." He turned to me. "Two glasses, I'm guessing, amigo?"

"Fine. Sure. Yeah. Amigo."

"And to eat?" he asked, weaving on the spot. "We've got some outstanding chorizo that would really lift the mood."

He had noticed the mood was flat.

"Later," I said, and flashed that terrible, fake British

smile again. Then I glowered at Sarah. "I've lost my appetite."

"Our calamari will bring it roaring back," he said, with a bounce of his eyebrows. Neither of us was looking at him anymore. Silence. "Cool, cool," he said, then left.

At the next table, no longer blocked by the waiter's presence, were four teenagers, lads — and in Britain, *lads* is a descriptive term — in athletic wear, two with their hoods up. Pints of San Miguel dotted their table.

"Who was it?" I asked, through gritted teeth.

"Just some guy," Sarah said, her face vacant, looking at me but focusing on my chin.

"Is this some sort of joke?" I asked her. "A prank?"

"What? What kind of joke would it be?"

I looked around at the tail end of long, boozy lunches. "Why would you tell me this here? In public?"

A ringtone. Crazy Frog. "Wazzzzzzzzzup," said one of the lads, answering a clamshell phone. His friends laughed. I moved my chair a little to the left, angled it away from them. A slight gesture that made no difference.

Sarah glanced at them, then back at me, then sobbed into her balled-up tissue. "I've spent weeks trying to understand why. It's why I've been... *off*."

I checked to see if anyone was looking at us. No one was.

"You should go," she said.

"But I just got here? I took a train. From Cambridge."

"You need to process this," she said. "It's a lot."

"Can't we do that together?"

Her head tilted. "Do you... want to?" She seemed genuinely surprised.

"Y-Yes? Isn't that what happens now? Normally, I mean. No?"

The waiter reappeared. Two glasses and a bottle in his hands. He put down the glasses. "Who's going to test?"

"*You*," I said, looking at Sarah. I didn't drink wine then. That wouldn't change until Evelyn.

"Lovely weather we've been having lately, right?" the waiter said, as he removed the cork inexpertly, the bottle between his legs. "Got anything planned for the weekend?"

"Hmm," Sarah said, quietly. "I might check out a music festival in Hyde Park."

I squirmed at the *I*. She'd never mentioned a music festival in Hyde Park. We used to spend every weekend together. I came to her and I also paid.

The waiter poured a small amount of wine into her glass. She gulped it down in one. Swallowed a burp. The waiter laughed. "Fair play."

"Fine," she said, gesturing impatiently for more, tilting her glass. He filled it half up, the wine sloshing around, staining the sides. He poured me a glass and I let him, because, well, whatever.

"Enjoy," he said.

Half a pint of beer fell over on the next table. The lads laughed uproariously and one jumped up, rushing to escape the golden river surging towards him. "Me trainers."

The waiter went to help. "Easssyyy, fellas," he said.

"I don't understand," I said to Sarah, who straightened, making firm eye contact now.

"You need to break up with me."

"But I don't even know what happened. Who was it, even?"

"Just some guy," she said in a whisper.

"You had sex with this 'some guy'?" I said, too loudly, and one of the lads looked over, sniggering. Sarah lowered her head, glugged her wine. "Don't I get to decide what happens next?" I asked. "Don't I get time to decide that? Tell me about it. About him."

"Why?" Sarah scowled, seeming genuinely confused.

"I want to know." I dropped my fist onto the table. "You owe me that, don't you?" I said, but I could hear my resolve cracking.

"Do I?" she asked, blowing her nose. She really didn't seem to have considered how this conversation might go, or that it might actually be a conversation. That I might want anything from her other than to just break up and leave.

"Oh my god," I said. "You want me to break up with you? That's the point of this?" I lifted my hands and looked around. "That's why it's happening here? In public?"

"Do I?" She chugged back the last of the wine in her glass. "I don't know. I just thought you would?"

"You do these things in restaurants if you want to avoid a scene. You wouldn't have done that unless..." I went silent.

She checked her phone.

"Should I go?" I asked irritably. "You got somewhere to be? Work?"

"I called in sick."

I put my elbows on the table and rubbed my forehead. "Are you sick?"

"Maybe. Look, you probably need some time," she said. "*We* do. I mean. To figure out what we want?"

"You've had weeks," I said. "What do *you* want?"

Her eyes circled. "I don't know."

"Well, it's not me then, is it?"

"I don't know, okay?"

"Who was it?"

"It doesn't matter."

"Tell me."

She looked at her phone again. "I don't have —" She

took a deep breath. "He's coming here. Okay. I'm sorry. But he is. I just..." She faded out.

"What?" I swivelled towards the door. "Why would you invite him here, now, while I'm here?" I laughed. I actually laughed. It was a wild laugh, not dissimilar to how I would laugh in the woods on day three, when my mind snapped.

"To talk about what happened," she said. "I didn't think you'd..." She rubbed at her temples with both hands. "I just assumed you'd leave. That you'd be disgusted with me and leave."

"I thought he was no one?"

She heaved her shoulders. "He must have been someone, I guess, for me to want to..." She lowered her eyes. "I need to understand what happened, too. I was happy. With you. *Us.* But then I can't have been, can I?" Her eyes were pleading, but I didn't know what for.

"What about me, though?" I asked, still unaware of what little control I had of the situation. "What about what I want?"

"What do you want?" she asked, but then said, before I could answer, "I mean, you probably need some time, right?" She looked at her phone. "It's not... He and I... It's just to talk."

I took a tentative sip of my wine, shuddered, and put it back down. "I feel like you're breaking up with me. No, that you've already broken up with me. But that you just didn't want to do it via text. So this was just supposed to be a quick formality."

The waiter returned, raising his thumb. "How we doing, team, I mean, ami —"

"Not now," I snapped. "Okay? Just fuck off."

"Adam," Sarah snapped, as the thespian slunk away, confused and offended. Two of the lads heard and stopped their conversation to listen. I slid my chair a little further away from them.

"Well," I said, quietly, "he had it coming. So fake. And then you invited me here as a formality, but allotted like five minutes for me? I mean, I'm an hour late. But that's trains. Trains are always an hour late. There are always leaves on the fucking line, aren't there? Because there are always trees near the lines. And why did *I* have to come here, anyway? Isn't it, like, etiquette that if you're going to break up with someone *you* do the travelling to them so that they can be at home and not have to go back to Liverpool Street and get another train that will be an hour late because of leaves on the sodding line?"

"You're babbling," she said. "This is a shock."

"If I want to babble, I'll babble, okay? What are you, the fucking babble police?"

The door to the restaurant opened. I saw it in the reflection of Sarah's recently refilled wine glass, the contents of which were rapidly being tipped into her mouth. Was this glass two? She twitched. A subtle twitch, but I knew her well.

I turned to the door, which was closing behind a man. He wore a rugby top — a salmon-coloured rugby top, collar folded up.

Physically, we were opposites. He was stocky, bald, his neck as wide as his potato face. He looked as if he'd grown up on a farm. Had opinions about which tractor manufacturer was the best: John Deere. Had been captain of his rugby team. Enjoyed Jeremy Clarkson. Drank Guinness for breakfast. Could name a dozen darts players.

Sarah flicked her head in a weird way. Obviously an attempt to signal him to wait without showing me he was there; it was unsuccessful.

The guy approached. "Hi," he said. He had a low voice, a smoker's edge to it.

"Can you just give us —" Sarah started, as I looked down at the table, begging it to swallow me up.

"Who are you?" he asked. She'd probably never told him about me. And why would she?

I didn't answer, being as I was already quite busy praying for the ground to swallow me whole.

"Toby," he said, holding out his hand to me.

I looked up at him but didn't shake his hand. "Adam," I said, bitterly. "The boyfriend."

"He's just leaving," Sarah rushed to say. "Call me in a few days, okay, Adam?"

It's weird when your partner uses your name. We didn't use each other's names.

"Boyfriend?" he repeated, chuckling.

Chuckling?

I stood up slowly, made it seem as if I were going to shake his hand after all, but then grabbed my glass of wine and, before I even knew what I was doing, threw the contents at him.

He saw it coming and ducked, showing admirable agility for such a lumpy man, and while half hit him in the cheek, the other half sailed past his cauliflower ears and splashed down onto the lads.

"What the fuck?" one said, leaping up. The rest of the table jumped up with him, blocking my way to the front door.

"Shit," I said, and turned and ran in the other direction. There was nowhere to run, of course, because this was a restaurant, not a school playground. I was moving past tables and towards the kitchen when I saw the sign for the toilet. The waiter was coming towards me, carrying a large tray with several plates of food, and I turned to slide past him but my foot caught on a chair leg and I stumbled forward and into him and he spun, dropping the tray and a glass shattered and plates banged and a cloud of food rained down, mostly oysters, foods equivalent of golf. I recovered my footing and was through the toilet door before they landed.

Down three steps. Look left. Look right. Two doors. Two figures. Small. One with a skirt. One with no skirt. Men's. Must be. I pushed on the door, heart in my throat, stomach gurgling. Inside, two urinals against the wall. At the back, a cubicle, floor-to-ceiling door. I rushed in and locked it behind me and as I did, my stomach exploded. I puked violently into the bowl.

As I vomited, I was up in my head again, floating as I had been in that bundle, thinking about how amazing it was that a body could react like this. That events of the world could make you feel so much that you vomit. It had never happened before.

The door to the toilets thudded open.

"Come out," said a booming voice. I heard several footsteps on the tiled floor. "*Now.*"

"Busy," I said. "Hang on."

A fist banged on the door.

"Where is he?"

"He's hiding."

"He's ruined my hoodie."

"It was a misunderstanding," said Toby, the man who'd helped destroy my wonderful, multi-year relationship by being so irresistible at an off-site, perhaps in his rugby top. "He was aiming for me. Well, he got me, too."

"Yeah, but the thing is, right, he's splashed my mate, ain't he? And we can't have that, can we?"

"And he's not even apologised, has he? The twat," said another voice.

Twat. The same insult one of the schoolyard bullies had used.

Someone kicked the door of the cubicle. "OUT!"

"He didn't mean it," said Toby. "He was aiming for me."

"Why are you defending him?" one of them asked. "Some nerd throws his drink at me and I'm going to smash it over his head."

"He's his mate, init."

"He's not my..." Toby said. "It's complicated. But trust me, he's having a bad day. Worse than you."

"It's about to get a lot worse for him, though, isn't it?"

My stomach gurgled, and I spat a last chunk of my breakfast into the bowl. Where was Sarah, I wondered? Why wasn't she here helping? Wasn't this her fault? It was the men's toilet, but there were no other customers in it. At least there were no worms around. I flushed, put the seat down, and sat. The sun from the window above the toilet warmed the back of my head. There was a little sick at the corner of my mouth and I was light-headed, scared, and confused. I reached over, grabbed two sheets of toilet paper, and wiped my mouth.

The window.

I turned. It was big enough. Not for her new lover but for scrawny, Ross-wannabee me. I stood on the seat and reached for the handle as the next blow hit the door. A shoulder? A foot? The hinges rattled. The window opened. Another thud.

"You're trapped, fella. Come out. Be a man about it."

Another shoulder barge. The door was shaking.

I stuck my head out the window. Ground floor. An alley. Just a sliver of sun making it over the top of the office building opposite. Vodafone. One leg in, one leg out.

I hesitated. If I did this, if I climbed out this window, I would be, officially, undeniably, for the rest of my life, the sort of desperate, devastatingly wimpy man who climbs out bathroom windows to avoid fights and breakups. It was embarrassing to flee, sure, but was it much more embarrassing than having your girlfriend cheat on you at a work retreat? I mean, what a trope. Not to mention having her break up with you without using those words and scheduling your replacement to arrive an hour later, wearing a rugby top.

Salmon coloured.

No, I reasoned, and grabbed the edges of the window frame and stepped through, turning and lowering myself. I fell onto my ass and got up and was running once again, head straight, shoulders back, chest full. Running as I had run that day on the school field, as I had run so many days from so many things. I didn't stop and I didn't look back and I jumped off the curb and forced a delivery van into an emergency stop as I skidded off its bonnet, bruising my hip, but there was no time for that.

BEEP BEEP BEEP

I saw a park and swerved into it and there — ignoring four perfectly good, perfectly empty red benches — I ducked behind a thick hedge that ran along the fence. I checked, couldn't see the street, and sat low with my back to the fence, no longer sure of anything much.

25

Evelyn materialised standing over me, half in the bush, her cheeks red, probably from embarrassment. She turned around and sat down next to me as much as she could in her snowy spectral form. "Is it over?" she asked.

"I was going to take them too, you know."

"Sure, honey."

"I had a plan and everything. I was luring them here."

"To hide from them?"

"Just the next stage of the plan. A complex, fiendish plan."

"Why did the plan not work out then?" she asked.

"I'm very good at hiding?"

"Apparently," she said. "But what did happen next?"

"Nothing, really. I just sat here for a while. Then I got up and went home. I just about made it back to Cambridge without vomiting again. I had to hang my head out the train window around Stevenage, but you could raise the property value of Stevenage with a bit of vomit. That's the one place you can guarantee there won't be any leaves on the line as they burnt all their trees for firewood years ago."

"Can you stop making jokes?"

"Do I have to?"

"What happened with them? Her and Mr Potato Head?"

"I... I don't know, actually? That was the end for us, although I remember quite a lot of embarrassing, grovelling texts and phone calls from my side. Not my finest month."

DING

"She was an idiot," Evelyn said. "And also, kind of plain, no?"

"Wow, that's kind of bitchy for you."

"Well," she said. "If she hurts you, she's my enemy."

"She was fun," I said.

DING

Evelyn laughed. "Too fun, yeah. Still, at least you didn't walk in on them having sex, like I did my ex." She was exaggerating, but I didn't correct her. "You left out the toilet bit, " she said, "when you told me this story. And that Toby came. And those dudes. Actually, kind of most of it, really." Her nose twitched. "Why?"

"Too embarrassing," I said. "Too wimpy. Too shameful."

DING

"She wanted you to break up with her," Evelyn said. "Nice and clean." She wiped her hands on her trousers. "Let you take the high road. She moves on, doesn't have to deal with the aftermath."

"Maybe," I said. "To be honest, I'm just really embarrassed that this is one of my so-called demons. It really wasn't that big of a deal. I know lots of people with way worse breakup stories. Even you have way worse breakup stories." I sighed. "I just want to have bigger trauma, I guess?"

"Think about that sentence again."

"You know what I mean, though, right? I want to leave this place and be able to explain to you, the real you, why I messed up my side of the last year. And more than that — why I detach emotionally from situations where I don't have control, why I defriend people as soon as they want something from me, why I'm a workaholic, why I didn't do more to understand what you were going through. Getting beaten up at school now and again and being cheated on, none of this stuff excuses any of that. It doesn't even feel related to most of it."

"I don't know," she said. "It must be, no?"

"Maybe it's just what's related to us?" I said. "To our issues?"

DING

"But then we need to understand its significance," I continued.

"You told me that having your heart broken was the greatest experience of your life," said Evelyn. "That you never felt so alive. I thought you were full of shit."

"It was like I learned a new language, for feelings," I said, of that heartbreak.

She shook her head. "Bullshit. No dings."

I bristled, or I would have, if I could have. "I'm not lying. I don't think I'm lying. Am I lying?"

DING

"Have you ever puked again from emotion?"

I considered it. "I've never even come close."

"That's strange, right?"

"Is it?" I said. "I mean, life gets less intense as you get older, right? You've already done everything so many times already. The novelty wears off. First loves are the most intense loves. As are first heartbreaks. This was the first big one." Her eyes narrowed. "I mean," I jumped to say, worried I'd offended her, "falling in love with you was one of the most intense experiences of my life. I could puke about you one day."

DING

She rolled her eyes. "That's not as romantic as it sounds. You really loved *her* more than you love me?"

I hesitated, which was its own answer. "There's still time," I said. "And you're pregnant. We're about to do a totally different thing. I want to love you more. I should love you more. And the kid. I want to love that kid as fiercely as my parents loved me."

DING

"We were spectacular," she said huffily. "Before the IVF stuff derailed us. I feel like you've already forgotten."

"Maybe," I said, to no dings.

"This must be about control too?" she guessed.

It made sense. Sarah had stolen our relationship from me and given it to someone else.

"To really love someone, you have to surrender control to them," I said, feeling it out. "And I haven't done that since this moment. Given control. Really loved. Not since Sarah."

DING

Evelyn lowered her eyes. I hadn't needed that ding. I'd known the answer was right. "This is the next evolution of *If I'm in control, I'm safe*. I doubled down. This is - *The less I feel, the less I can be made to feel*. Because if you can't control the world, you control your emotions, right? Shit. How stupid. It's not that life *has* to be less intense, necessarily, as you age — I've just made it so." It was a shame I couldn't move because I wanted to do something triumphant like pump my fists while shouting "Eureka!" "It's not that I loved her most. It's that I was capable of more love then."

"It's both really smart and really stupid," she said. "Sorry."

"I can change it. I'm going to change..."

The scene was already fading. My eyes closed, and when they opened, I was on my back on my mat, staring up at the ceiling, covered in sweat, as the room emptied around me. I lifted my hand to my face and wiggled my fingers and they reacted exactly as they should; I could control my body again. This had been a crazy, crazy experience, and it was only day six of ten. I needed a new vocabulary for the emotions I was experiencing here. At this moment, it was something in the general ballpark of but not quite awe. Awe that Evelyn had been so right. I don't know if she knew me better than I knew myself, but it was obvious now that I was ignorant of myself.

I settled myself on my knees, ignoring everything that hurt. I emptied my mind and moved my attention to my breath. After a few minutes, I concentrated on the little toe of my right foot to the exclusion of everything else. I fired a beacon at it, and although I was careful to have no hope or expectation or need or want or wish, a sensation answered.

TINGLE

It had happened. It had finally happened. My little toe had sparked with warm electricity. I was so shocked that I shrieked. It took a few seconds to calm down and get back to the breath then back to my toe, which was a raucous flesh party of sensations. It was real, this power, this technique. I swept across to the other toes on my right foot and then jumped the gap between my feet and into the digits of my left foot and the trail of sensations followed. It was like tickling myself from the inside with an internal lightsaber.

Up the legs.

To the knees.

The thighs.

I was giddy. It was actually real. I was going to new layers in my mind and discovering new layers to my body as well. Sensations everywhere, like stars lighting up the night sky of my consciousness.

I was going to be a father. I would never have control over my life, or Evelyn, or our child, and that was okay. It's impossible to truly enjoy life's gifts if you're constantly trying to assert your will upon them.

I swept and swept and swept and eventually reached the crown of my head. I didn't even notice the next session start and end because I had become a wizard, basically.

I had faced my demons and won.

26

Day 7/10: AM and PM
Location: The astral realm
Mood: Euphoric

Meditation had become a joy. Each sweep freed energy that galloped through the cells of my body like wild horses.

No matter where I was or what I was doing — walking the perimeter, sitting with my eyes closed on my cushion, lying in bed counting tiles — it was as if my whole body was pulsing with electricity. The effect was so pronounced I kept expecting other people to see it, too. That someone would come and throw a blanket over me because I was dazzling everyone at lunch.

I loved Vipassana. I loved meditation. I loved Buddhism. I even loved Goenka, sort of. I loved everything, I suppose, except golf.

"Don't play the game of sensations," Goenka cautioned, as I swept myself to ecstasy. "Pleasant sensation, negative sensation, big sensation, small sensation — makes no diffff-ferenCE."

Sorry, Goenka? Did you say something? I was busy over here being an epic wizard.

"Just observe, neutrally, your mind calm, still, and perfectly equanimous."

I CAN TICKLE MYSELF WITH MY THOUGHTS!

"Accept the reality of the present moment."

Vroom. Vroom. WIZARD!!

What was genuinely funny now was how little I wanted time to slip away. I would have gladly stopped it because each session was more exciting than the last with me entering some truly remarkable headspaces.*

I felt like an explorer gifted a whole virgin continent to map. I now understood why people might sit in a cave for years at a time, just inner sweeping.

I didn't broom for other men, but I gladly broomed for myself. My mind had far greater depth than I'd ever known. I was suddenly fascinated by the concepts of breathwork and psychedelics and ecstatic dance and lucid dreaming and Wim Hof ice bathing and, hell, maybe even therapy, I guess? Anything that might reveal more of these states. Anything that might lead me to extraordinary new locations in that unchartered continent.

I didn't like Goenka's methods, but he and the Buddha sure got results. I was speeding towards my salvation, right?

---

*You can go deep on this stuff, but Goenka never did, and it's dangerous to turn meditation into a personal bliss quest. You just need to know, should you be considering meditation, that there are a bunch of really-incredible-sounding states of ultra-heightened concentration where the material world fades away. They're widely reported and you can think of

them as rest stops on the way to the final state Buddhists call enlightenment. They're called jhanas and there are four, with the fourth divisible into four even subtler states. I feel confident I experienced the first two jhanas on this retreat, although since I didn't read about them until I got home, I'm relying on fleeting memories of short-lived states, so I won't distract from the main story to discuss them.

27

Day 8/10: AM
Location: The meadow
Mood: Jilted lover left at altar

Wrong.

The morning of day eight was difficult as the high of my... high wore off. I found it harder to focus on small bodily sensations as the novelty of them decreased. My mind, over which I'd had great mastery for a short while, felt it had learned all it could from these new states and, with nothing more to learn, bored of them.

Like a truck in the mud, I kept constantly slipping back as I tried to move forward with my mindfulness practice, as I tried to purify myself.

By late morning, I could no longer leash myself to the breath for more than a minute. Pain observed was not always pain halved. Thoughts, doubts, and a heckling voice returned to shout that I was stinky, sticky shit on humanity's expensive new shoes.

In the mid-afternoon, I was sweeping gleefully when the sensations stopped entirely, the strobe powering down with a dull whine. That was a bugger, really, and I didn't react to it maturely. I got petulant and sulky and, if I'm honest, stroppy and stompy. Had I not actually learned anything from my battles with my demons? Had all this self-torture been for toffee?

I didn't even like toffee.

I went outside and rubbed angry grooves into the dirt of the forest and the grass of the meadow like day three me — a person I'd hoped I'd slain. As I walked, I was accompanied by thoughts of my overwhelming inadequacy. I tried to disarm those thoughts, as Goenka had suggested.

"Hello, immense, engulfing sadness," I'd say. "Even though I feel like running headfirst into that enormous tree over there, you're going to pass and in five minutes I won't even remember that you were here because everything is impermanent. So, you know, your move."

That helped, I suppose, but the negative-thought loops were still there, and gaining strength. In the woods, I sat down on a knobbly tree stump and went back to the beginning, turning the soil of my mind over and over.

What had I learned so far?

I'm a control freak - have been ever since I was a child, when I had none, and lived in a place that didn't always like me.

I have a habit of running away — whether in school yards, restaurants during breakups, and emotionally when people need things from me that I fear I can't give.

These were my demons. They had haunted my life and my relationships and if I didn't defeat them once and for all, they would continue doing so into my fatherhood, and I couldn't have that.

What was I missing?

I let my mind wander and watched where it went. The breakup and bullying memories were rarely there now, perhaps because I understood the ramifications of them more, could watch them with an equanimous mind.

There was a third scene, however. It was the scene I'd seen most during the past eight days. The scene I'd found most disturbing of all. I'd been trying to avoid it at all costs. There were a few reasons for this:

1) I hadn't wanted to believe it was important.

2) I hadn't thought it was a demon because, unlike the other two, it hadn't actually happened, as far as I knew.

3) It was kind of kinky.

It was always there, looping, just like Willie Nelson. And that had to mean something, didn't it?

I thought about how Goenka had defined *demons*. Which was when I realised that he hadn't really, beyond that they were the things that unsettled our minds, that stopped us from meditating, that created strong saṅkhāras of craving or aversion.

By that definition, this scene was the biggest, angriest, meanest demon of them all.

And it was time to face it.

28

Thhhhwwwwuppp.

I opened my eyes.

Oh god, close, eyes! I don't want to see that!

I snapped my eyes closed and turned my head. I had come to in my thirty-six-year-old body, in our Berlin apartment, in the smaller back bedroom, the room that would become our child's room one day. It had been Evelyn's room when we first met, back when she'd had a roommate.

Evelyn was on the bed, moaning loudly. I went to cover my ears, which was when I learned my hands were restrained behind my back.

"Help!" I yelled, but my mouth was also covered and only a quiet, garbled sound came out. "Hhhlp."

I felt as though I were being sat on by an angry giant. Why was it so hard to breathe? My chest wouldn't expand. Someone was apparently crushing the sides of my head. I looked down. I was wearing a full-body black rubber bondage suit so tight it must have been sprayed onto me and sitting on one of the wooden chairs from our kitchen. From two anchor points — metal rings near my hips — chains looped behind and below me, securing my hands and feet, which I couldn't move. On my lap were three neatly folded pink towels and on top of them, a bottle of water-based lube. I appeared to be some kind of sex caddy.

On the bed, a metre away, her back to me, Evelyn was thrusting up and down, in the reverse cowgirl position, on the generously proportioned penis of a man whose face I couldn't see. The crown of his head was visible as he lay back. He had a lot of very messy black hair. He was moaning too. The third person wasn't even really involved yet — a blond who met every definition of Herculean. He was kneeling next to her, masturbating furiously.

I hadn't been this confused since *Lesbian Vampire Academy*. I had a powerful urge to vomit, which I had to suppress, since I had no way of vomiting and because Evelyn had already said my doing so because of her wouldn't be a compliment. I was here to look, I told myself, and so with my face angled away, I watched from the corner of my eye. It felt like holding my hand over a candle for eternity.

The men were composites of her two recent ex-boyfriends — based on snatches of what Evelyn had told me about how they looked and, I suppose, my own late-night feverish internet stalking. But my imagination hadn't stopped there, of course. It had dosed these men with all the world's steroids until they were the crispiest of man-crumpets, cheekbones like spanners and rippling, juicy pectoral muscles.

That was my woman, goddammit.

I had to stop this, but how?

"STOP!" I shouted, but they were having too much fun, were being too vocal. I swapped to a scream, but my stupid mouth-covering was muffling everything. I looked around. Could I reach something to throw or knock over?

I tried to move the chair, but my legs were secured too

tightly. I managed a little bunny hop. The lube? I thrust my hips and on my third attempt, the bottle wobbled and rolled and hit the floor, as did the top towel on the pile. I looked up, expectantly, but by now Evelyn, still facing away from me, had taken hold of the metal bars of the headboard, was gripping them as she thrust faster and faster, turning her head to passionately kiss this third man, their tongues like two eels in a sack.

No one seemed to need any towels.

Her moaning became a loud, guttural scream to the point of parody or, well, porn, which is kind of the same thing most of the time.

My woman. That was my woman.

I barked like a dog and hopped and wobbled and shook and, getting some rhythm going and with some preemptive bracing, managed to tip myself onto my side. There was an almighty crash and great pain arose in my shoulder and hip as the chains dug into me and it didn't pass away anywhere near as quickly as I would have liked.

Evelyn's moaning stopped. She turned her head. "Blimey," she said. "What have you come as?" She laughed, a trickle that became a flood. "Check him out, you two."

"I will not be laughed at by my imagination," I said, but it just came out as a long muffle. I tried a groaning, pleading noise.

"Hmmm?" she said.

"MSMSMFMSMSDMSMDSMDM."

"Carry on?" she said jokingly, reaching for the blond man's —

"NOOOOOO," I screamed.

She stopped mid-reach. "I was kind of close as well."

"STOPPPP!"

"Okay, okay," she said, climbing off the bed. "Chill out, gimpy." She wiped herself on a pair of blue boxers which lay on the floor near my head. "It's too much penis," she said. "Threesomes. No one needs that much penis. You know?" She turned, looking for something, and spotted it on the bars of the headboard. A set of keys. She undid a padlock behind my back.

My hands free, I reached up, feeling round the back of my head to whatever was restraining me. There was a zipper. I yanked it down and, spitting saliva and gulping for air, pulled off the mask, which was separate from the suit.

"*Ugh*. Yuck. Jesus Christ. That was torture."

"Eh," she said. "I've had worse. Have you been there the whole time?"

"What do you mean the whole time?"

"Foreplay," she said, and coughed.

"Not this time, no."

Her cheeks reddened. "Probably for the best."

"You're making jokes?" I said, swallowing more great gulps of air as she took hold of my arm and helped me up. "Seriously?"

"See," she said. "Now you know how it feels." Her face was flushed and her hair glistened with sweat. She righted the chair and I sat back down, shaking my arms, trying to wake them up.

"I'm not a ghost," she said, flapping her arms. "I can touch things." She looked back at the bed. "Kiss things."

I lunged for her, wrapping her in a hug, nuzzling into her neck. Her usual tropical coconut scent was mixed with that of cigarettes and aftershave. Her last boyfriend had been a smoker, I suddenly remembered.

"Hi there," she said, surprised, taking a half step back to not fall over. "Fine. *Okay*. I should probably get dressed though, right? And you out of that suit?"

She was wearing the same purple bra she'd worn that day she'd first scheduled sex in my calendar. The rest of her clothes were piled on a chair on the other side of the room, which at least meant no one had pulled them off in a fit of passion. She got dressed — in fitted black trousers and a black shirt covered with tiny white swans; a work outfit. If she was pregnant, she'd finally be able to leave that job.

"Can you help me?" I held out my arm and she grabbed the end of the sleeve and pulled.

"That's not it," she said, and went round to my back and undid several clasps and zips and tugged and pulled and yanked and somehow, we got it down to my waist. I had to sit on the chair again, and it took a prodigious amount of tugging to get my legs out. We were both out of breath by the time I was finally free.

"How do people wear stuff like this?" I asked. "I feel like removing jeans kills 60 percent of the mood. This is ten times worse."

"Only someone who's never worn a corset would say that. And you don't have to remove it," she said, pulling the groin zips and revealing the easy-access pouch built into the suit.

"Practical."

"And easy to clean. You can just hose it down." She stuck out her tongue.

"Ugh."

She went to the wardrobe and opened it. "If this is my room before you moved in, you should have clothes here." She reached in and then handed me a plain grey T-shirt and a pair of navy trousers. "Is the door locked?" she asked, then went to check. The handle rattled. "Door's locked. Okay, so it must be about this. It's more fun this time because I'm not a ghost and we're in a locked room. It's like we're playing an escape game. I'm good at escape games. The guys had massive shoulders," she said. "That a clue? Are you self-conscious about your shoulders?"

"I'm not sure the shoulders are where we should focus," I said, getting dressed, ignoring the fact that much of my errant attention during meditation had been devoted to the topic. "It's got to be about more than the shoulders, right?"

DING

"I feel like this one is pretty obvious," she said. "You're afraid you won't satisfy me sexually and I'll cheat on you."

I spent some time with the idea. "No, that doesn't feel right."

DING

"Do you feel you aren't enough for me, then?"

"I'm not enough for you, but I'm okay with that."

DING

"It's normal to be attracted to other people," I continued. "I want you to have every interesting experience you can. We're not here for a long time — we're here for a good time."

Her eyebrows lifted. "Where's that gem from?"

"It's something my granddad used to say."

"I think it's from a song."

"Maybe."

"How long did he live?" she asked.

"Until about ninety. Wasn't really true in his case."

"You've never talked about your granddad, right?" she asked. "I don't remember anything about him."

"He was your common, garden-variety lunatic. There's not much more to say about him than that."

"Ooookay," she said, taking a step back, towards the bed. "Let's focus. We solved the bullying and breakup by studying what was happening in your body. What did you feel when you were watching me?"

"Hmm," I said, sinking into myself, doing a sweep of the emotions there. "I felt everything all at once, in industrial doses — sadness, fear, disbelief, relief, resignation, vindication, arousal."

DING

"Arousal?" She frowned. "Why would you feel arousal? I thought this was a demon? A nightmare?"

I shrugged. "Why are some people turned on by balloons? Or their mother's perfume or rubber gimp suits?"

My eyes wandered around the room, to see what else might be wrong. The next time I looked at the bed, the men were gone. "Bed's empty," I said, bouncing my eyebrows, because if we could touch here, we could...

"They wore me out," she said. "And see, sex isn't an area where you lack confidence."

"I was thinking that, too. I'm actually pretty uncomplicated, as long as I feel broadly in control."

DING

I sat back down on the chair, closed my eyes, took a deep breath, and began a sweep from my toes upwards, just as I would in meditation, paying careful attention to each emotion, trying to see if I'd missed anything subtle. "It's not betrayal," I said, when I reached my chest.

"I didn't look like this as a child," she said. I opened my eyes to see her looking at photos on a shelf. "The nose is completely wrong. It's your nose."

"Forget that," I said. "It should be betrayal, right? The emotion? And it's also not jealousy or anger or any of the treachery emotions. Shit," I said, jumping up. "I just remembered something." I pointed towards the hallway. "On the day you surprised me with this retreat, you came out to the hallway and there was my sports bag there, full, and I thought you were going to kick me out and I remember I felt relief then, too."

DING

She scowled. "Why would you feel relieved if I had a

threesome without you? Or was going to kick you out of the house?"

I went and sat on the bed, running my hand across the silver duvet cover. It was warm. I waved her towards me. She sat down next to me, our feet on the floor, almost touching. I remembered a house party where we'd sat like this on the edge of someone else's bed, at the nadir of our relationship. I'd failed to understand what she was going through, and that failure stung mostly because, I realised now, I hadn't even tried to.

She gave me her hand.

"I think, maybe, if you did something like this threesome, or violated the rules of our relationship in some other big way, it would be over, right?" I said. "You would leave me no choice but to break up with you. Like Sarah assumed I'd want."

The ding took longer to come, as if deeper in my subconscious, dots were being connected.

DING

"That would be a relief to you?" she said, her voice rising.

"Apparently," I said. "Yeah?"

DING

"And if I lost you, I'd have control of my life again. There would be no infertility. There would be no sad partner. I wouldn't need to stay in Berlin, even."

"Yeah, but you wouldn't have me," she said, but I'd moved on to the next conclusion.

"I get it. My mind, or some part of it, actually wants you gone."

DING

A smile spread across my face. "These horrible images I've been seeing during Vipassana are actively trying to sabotage how I feel about you. Trying to push you away. It's not that I'm afraid you'll do this — it's that part of me deep down hopes you will. *Wow!* That's really messed up."

DING

She sucked air in through her front teeth. "That's horrible."

"It thinks it's helping me," I said, rubbing my head. She shrank into herself. I slipped my arm around her shoulder. "Obviously it's not helping. It's wrong. God, my mind is such a mess. I would never have guessed it was like this."

DING

"That's why the past matters," she said, "why the bullying and the breakups and whatever else percolating down here matters. Those rules you've made, *If you're in control, you're safe* and *The less you feel, the less you can be made to feel* have become scripts you don't even know you're following anymore. If your mind's trying to break us up, trying to get rid of me, we need to go deeper into your subconscious to change those scripts."

"Into Adamistan," I said, because I knew it was what she was thinking. "There is no Adamistan."

She waited. No ding. She grooved beside me, elbows out, knocking into me. "No ding, motherlicker. There *is* an Adamistan. It's no fun in my head, let me tell you," she said. "It's why I don't hang out there. You wouldn't live in your imagination all the time if it weren't a really fun place to hang out. Adamistan is where your ego lives. If we want to understand you, if we want to get to those scripts, if we want to understand more about how your mind works and how to change it, that's where we have to go."

"If it were an actual place, which it's obviously not, how would we get there?"

"The same way we got here. What else have you been seeing these past days? Any other demons? Loops? Clues? Places we can jump?"

"No," I said. "Not really." We sat in silence as I thought more about the jail I'd lived in for the past week. Were there more jailers? "I saw faces quite a lot," I said, eventually. "All the people I've defriended over the years. They took turns telling me what a world-class asshole I am."

DING

"Not one of your best traits," she said. "Your defriending. It's part of it, although I don't know how it connects yet. Were these memories or more like" — she swept her hand back towards the bed — "whatever this little erotic freak show here was?"

"Fantasies," I said. "Sometimes they would work together. One time they were an enormous group that chased me down a plane and I hid in a —"

"Good," she interrupted. "That's where we have to go. Shut your eyes and focus on what you remember from that."

"That's not going to work," I said, but I did as she instructed and closed my eyes, concentrating on the faces of the ghosts of my past, which was when I felt that same sharp pinch upon my consciousness. We were snapped backwards then fired down through many layers of my mind until we crashed into a plane toilet, of all things.

29

Evelyn and I materialised, in a tight embrace, standing on the closed toilet seat. I clicked my jaw, trying to clear my ears. "Wow," I said. "That was easy."

"Lucky the lid was down."

"Why would my happy place be a toilet?" I asked.

"Maybe everyone's subconscious is a toilet?" She pointed to a logo on the back of the door and laughed. I craned my neck around her to see.

Adamistan Air - you've probably seen a documentary about it.

The logo was a silhouette of my face. "Wonderful," I said.

"Uh-huh," she said. "They really got the nose right. All of it."

"Should we get down?"

"Yeah, me first. Hold my hand," she said, and stepped down to the floor.

"I hope our child doesn't get my nose," I said.

"Me too."

"Your nose is lovely."

"No," she said. "I meant your nose."

"Oh." I climbed down. "Right."

She disengaged the toilet's lock and the light overhead turned off.

"Let me go first," I said, unsure of what was waiting out there for us. She squeezed back against the sink and I slipped past her and pushed on the door gently, peeking out at what, from the few heads I could see, looked like a full plane. A man in a uniform approached. I shut the door and did some hyperventilating.

"What's out there?" she asked.

"I just saw someone, and he was, well, familiar."

The intercom binged. "Gentlemen, it's your pilot here. Adam Fletcher. I know you're enjoying the flight with Adamistan Air." He had my voice, but he was lowering it to sound more professional. "We're now beginning our descent into Adamistan, where the weather is, as always, a perfect twenty-two degrees Celsius. Sit back, relax, and enjoy my competence, which is vast. Thank me."

BING

"The whole of Adamistan is going to be just you," she said. "Isn't it?"

"It's not going to be just me," I said, and waited for my confirmation in ding form.

No ding.

"No ding," she said. "So, ha, you're wrong. Can we get out of here? It smells."

"It's going to be just Adams here?" I asked.

Again, no ding.

"There are no dings here?" I guessed, waiting idiotically for a ding that didn't come.

"Why wouldn't there be dings in Adamistan?" she said, tying back her hair with a grey band from her back pocket.

"And without the dings to ask, it's hard to..." I tsked, realising the issue. "We're at the bottom of my subconscious. There's no lower level to ask."

"Maybe," she said. "Now open the door."

I took a deep breath and pushed open the door. We were at the back of the plane. A very normal-looking plane. I walked up the aisle and Evelyn followed closely as I scanned left and right rapidly — every single head was bald or had thin, lank brown hair in various stages of balding.

"Evelyn," I whispered, turning back to her.

"They're all you," she said, looking around wildly. "Oh my god, they are all you. I was right."

"Hey," said an Adam in an aisle seat, getting quickly up. "How's it going?"

"Fine," I said, but he wasn't looking at me.

I stopped in the middle of the plane as a mid-twenties Adam, experimenting with a beard that just made him look homeless, got up and tapped Evelyn on the shoulder. "Excuse me," he said. "Are you looking for a seat? There's a seat next to me. Sit down. Tell me about yourself."

Several others were vacating seats. It was feeling as if it were feeding time at the zoo.

"They're staring," I said.

"Why, though?" she asked.

"You," I said, quickly opening the nearest overhead luggage bin. "You're my dream woman." I searched frantically, pushing aside bags and coats. "Which means you're the dream woman of all these Adams too."

I found a sick bag.

"I'm not wearing a sick bag."

"I'll poke eyeholes in it," I said. "Obviously."

The bag was too narrow. I threw it on the floor.

"There's a free seat here," shouted an Adam two rows back, patting an empty window seat.

"First time in Adamistan?" asked the Adam in the aisle seat next to Evelyn, getting up.

I rummaged in the next bin, knocking more bags and suitcases out of my way. Did I have any reason to fear myself? After all, I knew how little I was capable of. I found a large blue hoody with an *Adamistan Air* logo on it.

"Put this on," I said, and she did, putting up the hood to hide her hair. I took off my glasses and gave them to her. They proved ornamental, I saw just as well without them.

"That enough?" I asked, looking around. "To stop a riot?"

"Seems to be," she said.

An Adam in the row in front of me got up from his aisle seat and walked to the front toilets. Only the window seat was occupied in his row, so I sat down in the middle, pulling Evelyn into the aisle seat.

"Keep your head down," I said.

"No one's over forty," she whispered. "Have you noticed that? And where are the children? The youngest Adam is what, sixteen?"

"The age I left school."

I turned to the Adam in the window seat. He was an early-thirties Adam. I recognised his trousers, which were shiny and a mistake and someone would shout "Oi oi fancy pants" at him out of a car window and he'd lose confidence in them then throw them away. He'd been leaning over surreptitiously to listen to our conversation.

"Why is no one over forty?" I asked him.

He lifted himself up with the help of both armrests and looked around. "I hadn't noticed."

"They're all about our age."

He scowled. "I'm not your age."

"You're like five years younger than I am."

"Exactly."

"Fancy pants," I mumbled.

He looked down at them. "Thanks?" he said, but doubt had crept into his voice like a thief in the night.

"What is Adamistan like?" I asked him.

"Paradise," he said, and took his notepad out of the seat pocket, flipping to the next free page. "Your first time?"

"Kind of."

"Make a lot of notes. Could be a good book in it, you know? Your classic fish-out-of-water story. Or a fish returning to water?"

"Details," I said, dismissively, and he laughed.

"I was going to say that."

A young Adam came down the queue holding up brightly coloured packets. "Sherbet?" he shouted. "Sherbet, anyone?" He was wearing three necklaces and six leather wristbands. I'd forgotten about this short-lived era. I'd just escaped my hometown to go to a college thirty miles away, which felt like three thousand, and I'd celebrated by experimenting with all popular subcultures at once, becoming a skate-punk-surf-yogi-frat-grunge-metal-hippie-goth-jock.

"You had acne," Evelyn said. "I didn't know that."

"Went away when I was about seventeen. Do you think the young Adams have menial jobs and then somewhere around thirty they all become writers and never do a hard day's work again?"

"A society full of writers?" she said, her voice full of horror. "Who'd do actual work getting dirty and bending and using power tools?"

"I hate bending," I said.

"Me too," said an Adam in the row in front, who'd also been listening.

"Excuse me," I said, "this is a private conversation." I leaned closer to Evelyn, lowering my voice. "Why would we need to go on a plane to Adamistan?" I asked. "Why didn't we just appear there?"

She fastened her seat belt. Not that we'd felt the plane move even once. "You're a travel writer," she said. "Planes are very significant to you, right? Your mind knows that all great journeys start with a plane ride."

I bit my lip. "I suppose, yeah?"

"Have you been watching out the window?" she asked.

"Nothing ever changes. It's the same completely clear patch of blue sky. It's like a poster."

"Maybe this is Adamistan?" she said. "Like, maybe it's just this plane and it never arrives?"

"Oooh," I said. "I like it. But it's a bit too clever for my imagination."

"Yeah," she said. "Nothing subtle about those dings."

Some sort of border-guard Adam came down the aisle in a large, pompous hat four sizes too big for his head. It wobbled as he walked. He stopped to check every aisle and paused for a long time next to Evelyn, his head tilting more and more as the seconds passed. "Name," he barked.

"Ev-Adam," she said in a fake deep voice.

"Birthdate?"

She said it without hesitation.

"Name of middle school?" he asked.

She said that too.

"Thank me," he said, and carried on down the aisle.

"I think this plane is fake," I said. "It's more like a holding area. They're checking that only Adams get in and maybe only certain Adams, too?"

There was a tap on my shoulder. It was an Adam in the row behind me, holding a notepad. "Couldn't help but hear you two Adams are new? What're your first impressions? I'll take it all. Funny's better, of course."

"Not now," I said. "And this is a *private* conversation."

"Right. Right," he said, as if it had been his idea to end the conversation early.

"Where are you travelling from?" I asked the Adam next to me.

"Little place called Berlin," he said. "You been?"

I chuckled. "Once or twice. Is the airport near Adamistan?" I asked.

"There's no airport."

BING

"Gentleman, I'm sure you'll have noticed that we have now landed, and perfectly. It's been your pleasure to have me on board today, and please stop by the cockpit on your way out to tell me what a great job I did. Thank me."

"Bit needy," Evelyn joked. "Did you feel us descend?"

"No," I said, looking around. "I didn't feel the plane bank even once."

BING

"Adams," said a young flight-attendant Adam by the door, phone to his ear, "it was your pleasure to be served by me today, and you hope you'll see me again soon. Please remain seated until the pilot has switched off the *Pretend you've fastened your seat belt when actually you've just laid it across your lap in a pointless gesture of independence* sign. Thank me."

I looked down at the seat belt I had pretended to fasten but had actually just laid across my lap in a pointless gesture of independence.

"Finally," said Window Seat Adam, moving the seat belt he had pretended to fasten.

Everyone was getting up out of their seats, opening the overhead bins — a free-for-all as Adams haggled, pushed, and persuaded their way past each other.

"None of them can queue," she said. "Just like you."

"Could I just squeeze past you there, mate?" said

Window Seat Adam, bent like a tree in high wind to avoid hitting his head on the air nozzles above his seat. "It's just I've got a short connecting flight. And I'd hate to miss it. Got people waiting for *me*."

There was something about the emphasis he put on the last word in the sentence, as if saying it hurt. He was lying.

"Oh, you don't live in Adamistan?" I asked.

He shifted on the spot, as much as was possible. "Oh, well, yeah? Normally. I'm just transiting today. So can you just slide across so I can slip past, pal?"

"No," I said, because I wanted to get Evelyn out of this plane before people noticed she was a she, not a me.

The first Adams were disembarking now. We moved into the aisle. I felt like a novice gladiator waiting to enter the Colosseum. I lowered my head as we left the plane. I could now see it had no wings or wheels. It was parked right next to what looked like an ornate city wall. From this height we could see over it, into a desert. In the distance was a small tent city.

I pointed at it. "What's that?" I asked the Adam behind me.

"The defriended live there," he said. "Don't go there. They attack us."

"There's a giant gold statue of you," Evelyn said, pointing in the other direction, into the city, which was a busy mess of bustling streets and wildly clashing architectural styles. The statue was clearly a rip-off of the Statue of Liberty. I didn't need to get any closer to know that the book I was holding was one of my own.

"And an enormous, glowing Buddhist temple," I said.

"And a Ferris wheel."

I rubbed my hands together. "This is going to be so great."

"Hmm."

30

We stepped down onto a street called, imaginatively, Fletcher Boulevard. Looking down it, I immediately recognised patchwork sections of buildings — there was a cathedral from Norwich, terraced housing from my student days in Nottingham, and a bustling market from Bangkok.

Everywhere I looked there were Adams, dozens of them, walking, running, scooting, biking, and eating ice cream cones as big as their fists. Adams were crammed into every nook, and the stationary ones were all smashing at their laptops or scribbling in their notepads, their faces tight rags of concentration, pondering their next great sentence.

We passed a bookstore called Fletcherstones. Its window display featured all my books. "Just look at it," I said. The shop was open but no one was inside. "Can we go in?"

"No," she said. "You're already aroused enough."

Somehow, Evelyn was passing as an Adam. I guessed, as with colour, what we see is mostly behind our eyes. And here, in a world full of Adams, there was no reason to look at anyone closely.

We walked towards a square, strolling down the

broad, carless road. The only businesses were bookstores, Indian restaurants, and sweet shops. We passed a football pitch, but no one was engaging in team sports. A few joggers lapped, alone, in their big DJ headphones. Every twenty metres was a water fountain. I stopped to drink at one.

"'High water needs'," Evelyn said, quoting me mockingly. I never left the house without water, even in winter.

The square was like the one on the street where we lived in Berlin, only there were large advertising screens paying some poor homage to Piccadilly Circus.

Carry on and you'll keep calm flashed up on an enormous screen.

"Shouldn't it be 'Keep calm and carry on'?" Evelyn asked.

"No," I said. "This makes more sense to me."

We sat on a bench to Adam-watch. Evelyn smirked with amused detachment while I felt as if I were singing naked in a football stadium as the halftime show.

"Evelynistan is very different," she said. "More of your classic Dante hellscape."

"You're always very harsh on yourself," I said, nodding.

"It's the easiest way to stay honest."

"Am I honest, do you think?"

She shook her head emphatically. "That's what all this is about. That's why we're here. Your self-confidence," she said. "Where do you think it comes from?"

Another sherbet seller passed, this one pushing a "ye olde" wooden cart.

"I know that there have been periods in my life where people thought little of me," I said, eventually cobbling together a theory. "If that happens, you have two choices, right? You can decide that they're right or that they're very wrong."

"Makes sense," she said, putting her hand on my thigh and squeezing.

"What should we do?" I asked.

"What do we normally do when we travel? Hang out, talk to people, and draw sweeping, poorly researched conclusions."

"Okay," I said, as an Adam approached us, his notepad out.

"I hear you two Adams are new," Adam said. "Got anything I can quote? I'm writing a book. It's going to be great. A classic."

"What's it about?"

"Everything. All of it." He nodded proudly. "The whole damn human sausage."

"It's about you, isn't it?" Evelyn joked.

His cheeks reddened. "It's got universal themes."

Two nearby Adams were sauntering down the pavement in exactly the same carefree way I sauntered places until about a year ago. "But you can make an exception for me, right?" said the first.

"I saw a documentary about it," the second replied.

"There's a good book in that."

"Do you have any chocolate?"

Another Adam stopped them. "Any good stories?" he asked. "I could use some material."

"I think I saw a documentary about it."

"Got any chocolate?"

"Does it get boring here if everyone is you?" I asked the Adam sat on the bench next to us dipping his finger into a packet of sherbet.

He scowled. "What do you mean everyone is me?"

I waved my arms around. "Everyone is me. You. *Us*."

He looked around. "These chumps are nothing like me."

"You're identical, pretty much, just different ages, but also not even, really."

"No way," he said, puffing up his chest. "I'm destined for greatness."

"Can you help —" I started to say.

His smile collapsed into a frown. He looked as if someone had served him food he was deathly allergic to. "I've enjoyed our time together," he said, jumping up and running away into Fletcherstones.

"I was only going to ask him for directions to whoever is in charge." I rubbed my head because I was having feelings. Intense feelings. I looked up at the slow-turning Ferris wheel. "Singapore," I said. "I knew this place was familiar."

"I've never been to Singapore," Evelyn said.

"It's a hellhole."

"It looks like this?" She seemed dubious. "It's a very spotless hellhole."

"It's what my mind remembers Singapore looking like. But Singapore is spotless. That's part of why it's a hellhole."

"I've never heard you talk about Singapore," she said, again offended I had denied her one of my opinions.

"It's one of my least-favourite countries on earth."

"Then why would you make Adamistan look like Singapore?" she asked. "And what's so bad about Singapore?"

I clicked my jaw. "It's a *Truman Show* country, only they've banned Truman from doing anything interesting. I saw a sign there once. You'd be fined about a thousand dollars if you rode your skateboard through an underpass. The whole place is like that. This glib surface hiding a weird, authoritarian, low-tax dystopia. If golf were a country, it would be Singapore. I can't believe my subconscious is Singapore. This is what wanting too much control creates. This place is horrible. You just don't see it at first." I sighed. "Narcissism runs in my family. Both my uncles are narcissists. And my crazy granddad was too. It makes sense that the safe place of a narcissist would be a world populated by only themselves, right?"

"Yes," she said. "It would."

I flapped my arms. "That's so sad. All of this is so sad." I listened for sounds of Adams enjoying themselves, but there were none. There was little conversation happening anywhere. Occasionally monologues were overlapping, but that was it.

I choked back a sob and all the Adams nearby stopped.

"He's losing it!" someone shouted. "Help!"

Adams rushed over. Evelyn looked unsure about whether she needed to jump in and defend me from all the Adams circling us now.

"Out, out, out," they shouted, pointing back towards the plane.

"Get out."

"Leave."

Several of them grabbed me and pulled me up then tried to push me from the square. Is it still peer pressure when your peers are you? I felt the pressure, regardless.

I straightened. Swallowed the emotion. Apologised. Thanked them all for their kind attention. They kept pushing me anyway. Three police Adams arrived on white scooters — the same scooter I owned.

"He's having an excess emotional event," an Adam shouted, but calmly. "Arrest him, Officer."

"There's a good book in this," another said, making notes.

In the scuffle, Evelyn's hood had come down.

"She's not an Adam!"

"Stay back!" I shouted at the crowd.

"Run," she said.

There was the screeching of tyres. We turned, fighting back the Adams.

"Here," a voice shouted from a vehicle on the other side of the square, just beyond the iron railing — it was a tuk-tuk. We ran towards it. The mob of Adams gave chase, as did the police Adams. Evelyn and I vaulted the railing and the tuk-tuk driver gunned the engine. The tyres squealed as Evelyn jumped inside and I chased it, lunging for the bars on its side and then leaping. I fell into the footwell as the tuk-tuk careened around the edge of the square and down Fletcher Boulevard, scattering Adams like bowling pins, Evelyn holding me so I wouldn't fall out.

"What the fuck was that?" I said.

"You disturbed the peace," said our saviour, an Adam in the same type of brown uniform Evelyn and I had worn during our tuk-tuk race across India. We were in Winnie, our beloved tuk-tuk. I gave her a quick stroke. She was a big part of our love story.

"Peace is overrated," I said.

"Don't tell these squares that," Tuk-Tuk Adam shouted back at us, throwing a loose thumb over his shoulder. Tuk-tuks have tiny, weak, loud engines. The wind whipped in as he sped up. Behind us, there was the sound of sirens. Evelyn slipped her hood back up. "Don't worry," he said, changing gears, the engine clunking. "I know a place we can hide."

"Why are you helping us?" I shouted at him as we skidded around a roundabout.

"Great material," he said. "I'm writing a book."

"Oh," I said. "I thought because it's the right thing to do?"

"Sure," he shouted. "That too."

We whizzed through busy streets where Adams plotted to have their genius recognised by the fickle people of the controlled hallucination we call reality. We were getting closer to that Buddhist temple. It was far bigger than I'd realised, looming large enough to block out the sun. It looked like something from an Indiana Jones movie.

"Is anyone in charge here?" I shouted at Tuk-Tuk Adam. We'd only just arrived, but I already wanted out. "Is there, like, a boss? Or some kind of, I don't know, control centre?"

"Yes," he said, pointing to the temple. "And that's where we're going."

31

The tuk-tuk skidded to a stop just in front of the temple, which was covered in thick vines and vegetation. Adam checked his mirror and flashed us a smile with all the same crooked teeth I had. "I did a great job, right?"

"You did, yes," Evelyn said.

"Really got you out of a jam."

"Yes," I said. "Thanks."

"Don't mention it. Unless you want to?"

"Are they coming?" I asked, looking over my shoulder.

"Yeah," he said, and pointed towards the pyramid. "You need to go up there, and quickly."

Evelyn and I ducked out of the tuk-tuk. "Will they follow us?" I asked.

"No one goes up there," he said.

Chunky electricity cables vines were glowing in the same dark shade of red as the pyramid itself. It was as if it was throbbing with energy. "It's a power station, isn't it?" I asked him.

"Something like that, yeah," he said, slipping the tuk-tuk into gear and peeling away. "Thank me!" he shouted.

Sirens.

We ran for the first step.

"I sort of hoped my subconscious would be post-stairs," I said, as we started up. The steps were almost vertical and covered in prickly vines and lush, sticky vegetation. The temple seemed to have its own climate. We were climbing each step in the most literal sense of the word, scrabbling up with our hands and feet. The humidity was stifling.

"You must be really trying to hide whatever is up there," Evelyn said, huffing and puffing as she held up a thick vine for me to slide under.

Thirty minutes later, wheezing from the exertion, we crawled over the top step and collapsed onto our backs. "Never... again," I said, coughing into my fist. The air was noticeably thinner up here. All the various Adams below were just little bald pinheads scurrying about in their clean, ordered megalomania. There was no sign of the police that had been chasing us for breaking the peace. Overhead, an eagle soared. I was afraid to look at it too closely, in case it had my face.

Behind us was a single-story stone building fronted by a square arch with no door. Above it, in that same childish handwriting that had been on my tray in middle school, were the words *The Great Wisdom Library of Adamistan* — the t's were uncrossed.

"Oh god," Evelyn said.

"Uh-huh."

Inside the building, the temperature plunged. I blew onto my hands as we walked along a narrow passageway which opened into an austere room with bare walls and bright strip lighting. Fifteen metres away stood four beat-up, dented metal filing cabinets. They looked as if they'd fallen from a plane, and perhaps they had. There were about fifteen drawers per cabinet and each one had a strip of labelled duct tape across it. The writing was in black pen and my childish scrawl. To the right of the cabinets, a young Adam sat on a fold-out camping stool, his head resting against a cabinet, sleeping. He was in my middle school uniform. The polo top's collar was ripped, as was the knee of his charcoal-coloured trousers.

We moved closer, and our footsteps on the concrete floor woke him up. He jumped up in shock and rubbed at his eyes. His glasses were missing. "Who goes there?" he said, in a put-on bass voice fifty years too old for his eleven-year-old body. It echoed off the ceiling.

"Err... it's me?" I said, and then turned to Evelyn, who had taken off her hoodie and glasses during the climb. "Well, us."

"An Adam," he said, disappointed. "You're intruding."

"*The* Adam," I corrected.

He bristled. "Any self-respecting Adam would say the same. You, however." He smirked at Evelyn. "You I know well." He ran his tongue across his lips.

"How do you —"

"It's wonderful to have you here at last, sweet Evelyn."

She looked around. "Err... yeah, what is this place, exactly?"

"This," he said, with a sweep of his tiny, hairless hand, "is the Great Wisdom Library of Adamistan."

"I think Alexandria's was bigger," she said, turning up her nose. "Just saying. No offence."

He puffed out his chest. "It's small, but I think you can see that it's perfectly formed?" He pulled out a drawer from the fourth cabinet, the one nearest to where he was standing. "In each drawer, a great wisdom. The combined wisdom of the Adams. Touch nothing."

"Oh, you're like a librarian?" I said.

"Incorrect," he boomed, as if nervous that those in the

cheap seats wouldn't be able to hear. "I am the custodian of the Great Wisdom Library of Adamistan."

I turned to Evelyn and whispered, "My mind is run by a bullied eleven-year-old? Actually, that explains a lot."

"I have so longed to meet you," he said to Evelyn. "You are part of so many of the most-recent wisdoms."

"What is that wisdom?" she asked, pointing to the open drawer.

He looked down at it. "A minor wisdom," he said, shutting it. "There are many excellent ones here. Let me see..." He searched frantically up and down.

She stepped closer to read the label on the drawer he'd closed. *"We're here for a good time, not for a long time,"* she read. "Can I see that one?"

"Is but a minor wisdom," he said. "Let me take you to something more profound. One of the many wisdoms learned from you, for example?"

We stepped even closer, crowding him. Reluctantly, he reopened the drawer. He was barely tall enough to see the inside, which was padded with purple velvet. On a raised purple cushion sat a bubble inside which a memory played. I recognised the bubble from the long, winding meditation queue.

"It's a pre-thought," I said.

He tutted. "No. A wisdom. More of a post-thought than a pre-thought."

"You can watch them," I said to Evelyn. "They play scenes. I know them from meditation."

She craned her neck to see. "In this one there's a bald man, and he's —"

"That's my grandfather," I said. "He's chasing pigeons in his garden."

"Why?"

"He wants to make a pigeon pie."

"He's run inside to the front door now," she said, as if I weren't watching too. "There's someone there. He's opening the door. Where are you in this memory?"

"In the living room."

"Why's he lifting his top up like that?"

"He's showing this man how he's been cut in half four times."

"On his doorstep?"

Librarian Adam looked similarly embarrassed by this memory and turned away, slipping his thumbs into his belt.

"Does he know the man?" she asked. "What's he doing now?"

"He's telling him how he was given a week to live when he was thirty. Now he's challenging him to an arm wrestle."

"He's wearing two hats, isn't he?"

"Yes," I said, but I couldn't watch anymore either.

Librarian Adam snapped the drawer shut and ran his hand down the front of the cabinet. "*If at first you don't succeed, post-hoc rationalise,*" he said, and gave a little clap. "That was a fine one, Evelyn."

"I said that?" she asked, turning from him to me. "I don't remember. Can I see it?"

He slid the drawer with the corresponding label open.

"It's us at the clinic," she said. "I forgot I even said that, the end to your sentence. It was such an intense day. So many forms and questions. But why would that be here? It was just a throwaway line."

"I liked it," I said. "And it's true, I think? I mean, I interpreted it as 'don't be afraid to take risks as your mind will post-hoc rationalise your failure away'. Not sure it would have worked for infertility. That one might have been too big for us both."

"Okay," she said. "I don't know if that's how I meant it, but who am I to say that your beliefs are faulty?"

"You will find no fault in the wisdom of the Adams," Librarian Adam said, with great pomposity.

"How long you been up here, kid?" I asked.

"I am not a kid. I am the wisest Adam of them all. No one has studied our scripture like me."

"Hmm. Uh-huh. Fine. The cables," I said. "Down on the street there were these thick power cables glowing red that ran into the temple. Do they connect to these cabinets? Is it all this that powers Adamistan?"

He shifted on the spot. "Not exactly, no."

"What then?" I asked.

"It is a secret."

"From myself? You're going to deny me my own knowledge?"

"Well," he said, and nibbled his bottom lip.

"I'd really like to know too," Evelyn said. "If it's no trouble?"

That helped. "Follow me," he said, eventually. "But DO NOT touch anything."

He led us behind the filing cabinets, where, at hip height, there was a glass case also glowing a faint red. In the case was half a worm.

"Spite," he said. "Turns out to be the most potent energy source in the universe."

I gasped. "Unbelievable. This built all that down there?"

"Yes," he replied. "Evelyn, would you like a private tour of the wisdoms?"

She took a step back. "Err, I'm pretty busy right now. I think we're just going to learn some things and then get the hell out of" — she giggled nervously — "lovely Adamistan."

"How long have you been up here?" I asked him again.

"Challenging to say. Time passes rather oddly here."

"Time dilution's a real bitch."

"Anyway," he said, with a high chin. "I enjoy it here. No one bothers me."

"What's that machine over there?" Evelyn asked, pointing to the wall near where we'd come in. "Looks like it's connected to the cabinets by another power cable?"

The machine had a sort of seismograph running across the front, its needle jumping up and down. It spit out reams of paper as lights whirled and flashed. Someone in the 1950s might have imagined a computer looking like this in the year 2000. Occasionally it stopped, as if it had completed some kind of complex equation, before whirring back to life again.

"The dinger," he said. "It dings."

"Ah," Evelyn said with a laugh. "We know about the dinger."

"The wisdoms are guiding the dings," I said, scratching my chin. "That makes sense, I guess? Before, I thought the dings represented truth, you know? That they were impartial. But if they're just based on beliefs, they're not more accurate than anything else, I think." I turned to Librarian Adam. "Can you open *If I'm in control, I'm safe*?"

He crossed his arms. "That one is closed right now."

"Why?"

"Maintenance?"

"Come on, kid."

"I'm not a kid."

"You don't like that memory, do you?"

He lowered his chin. "No Adam does."

"Open it."

Evelyn gently touched him on the elbow. He jumped in shock, and she used that shock to gently nudge him aside. We walked back round to the front of the cabinets. It was on the far left, near the bottom.

We watched it together, she and I, side by side.

Librarian Adam returned to his stool and swung his legs back and forth, staring down at the ground. "I was about to best them," he said, when it had ended. "I was lulling them —"

"Into a false sense of security," I said. "Sure you were, kid."

"Do you think this was the day I founded Adamistan?" I whispered to Evelyn, covering my mouth with my hand.

"Yes," she said. "The day you left your body and started hiding in your head. I thought it was wrong to rush to the conclusion that the worm demon was about control," she said. "I was trying to make you wait, but you'd left already."

"What else could it be?" I asked.

"Err?" She tapped the drawer marked *The only person you can rely on is yourself.* "Want to bet what memory is in the origin of that one?" she asked, opening it.

It was the worm memory again. She shut it triumphantly. I ran my gaze down the cabinet on the far left until I saw *Respect has to be earned* — my problem with authority.

I opened that. Worm.

Four drawers below that was *It's because you're so special that they attack you*, and one lower, *Deep down you are unlovable, and you must hide this.* "Same scene," I said, feeling my legs buckle. "Got another of those stools?" I asked Librarian Adam.

"That has not been necessary," he said. "And you'll be leaving soon, so..." He looked up at Evelyn. "You are most welcome to stay, of course. We have much to discuss and, I suppose, explore together."

I slumped down to the floor, my back to the cabinet. Evelyn sat down next to me.

"They're not wisdoms," I said. "They're beliefs. Well, misbeliefs, really. We were treating it like it was an escape game. That each demon was a clue that would lead to the next clue and, in the end, I'd sort of solve myself, but why would that be possible? Why would trauma be neat like that?"

"That's why there are multiple beliefs that come from the worm experience," she said, nodding. "And some of them are contradictory."

"It's all a big random soup," I said, and closed my eyes, trying to process everything I was feeling. Trying to assemble all the pieces of this. Things happen to us, both good and bad. From these events, we create beliefs that are parts of our larger models of the world. These beliefs try to help us navigate the world better. But the world resists navigation, is too complex for these simple reductions. The wisdoms, the models we build from them, are always wrong, but they're often helpful, and mostly work, so we don't abandon them. The more we follow them, the more automatic following them becomes. Evelyn was right to call them scripts.

I got up. "How do we remove" — I considered my wording — "wisdoms no longer serving the Adams?"

Librarian Adam got down off his stool, his bottom lip trembling. "They cannot be removed. They are sacred."

"Nothing gets removed?"

"No," he said, knitting his eyebrows. "Well, the less you think of them, the less weight the dinger assigns them in decision-making. It's very elegant. Would you like to hear more about the work, Evelyn? You are more beautiful than even the bubbles had me believing."

"Steady on, dude," I said.

He giggled nervously. "Have I been too forthright? Sorry, I am unpractised in the social arts."

"It's cute," she said. "Don't worry."

He blushed. "Thank you."

"Evelyn." I cleared my throat. "I think I left something outside by the stairs. A wisdom, maybe, even probably?" I hooked my head towards the door. She got the hint; not that it was subtle.

We walked outside.

"What's up?" she asked, when we were warming in the sun.

"This little nerd is proper creepy," I said.

"He's eleven."

"Got a real sketchy, underwear-off-the-washing-line-stealing kind of vibe about him."

"He's eleven," she repeated. "I think he's cute."

"You know what I'm thinking?" I bounced my eyebrows. "Let's blow this place the fuck up."

"The Great Wisdom Library of Adamistan?" she said mockingly.

"Yeah," I said. "All four filing cabinets' worth." I pointed down. "And Singadamapore too. Or at least let's blow up the city walls and let in those people stuck out in the desert. I don't want to live in a weird little world full of myself where the past is hidden and intense emotion is banned."

"Wouldn't you have to start again, though? Without all your wisdoms?"

"Yeah," I said. "But that doesn't sound so bad to me. A clean slate ready for parenthood."

Her mouth twisted. "How would we do it?"

"You distract him," I said. "And I'll make some changes up here."

"How am I going to do that?"

I angled my head and pursed my lips.

"What?"

I angled my head more.

"What?" she said. "I'm not getting it. Just use words."

I tutted. "Use your wily feminine charms, obviously.

This guy is hornier than a frat house on a Friday night. His tongue falls out of his mouth every time you give him even a little side-eye."

"He's eleven."

"Just lavish him with a bit of attention. Open your top button."

Her shoulders sagged. "I'm not a prop."

I wafted my hand. "Fine. Whatever. When we go back, laugh at his jokes or ask him to show you where the magic happens or whatever. Just buy me five minutes to trash his shitty library and blow up the city."

She sighed. "You're going to break his heart."

"Life already broke it. That's why he's hiding up here. I'm going to set the little weirdo free."

We walked back inside, hand in hand. "I still don't understand the *We're not here for a long time* one," Evelyn said. "The others I get — they came from a significant moment. But that one was just from your granddad being crazy and annoying someone at his front door?"

"The gene is in my family. I'm terrified that one day my mind is just going to snap — before I've proved all my doubters wrong and created something of real value."

"Spite," she said, and laughed.

"I think that fear is why I'm in such a rush. Why I'm a workaholic. My books are my little immortality projects, stupid as that is."

"Having a kid is pretty good for that," she said, nudging me with her elbow. "Immortality, I mean. Well, as much as anything is good for immortality."

"Yeah, but what if the kid gets my genes? I think some months I was secretly happy you didn't get pregnant. Because what if the kid is ill or wears too many hats or has my nose?"

"The genes on my side are great," she said. "Tip-top."

"I know. I checked them out very early."

"So," she said, and hugged me. "It's going to be okay. Or it's not, and that will have to be okay too. There's more craziness in your family than mine, but there's also more love. And anyway," she said, laughing, "we're here for a good time, not for a long time, right?"

I smiled. "Right. Well, right enough. Now let's watch this world burn."

We walked towards the filing cabinets. Librarian Adam was busy dusting with a long bright-red feather duster.

"Did you find the wisdom?" he asked.

"Yes," I said. "I think so."

He was dusting the drawer with *The less I feel, the less I can be made to feel*.

"That's the breakup with Sarah, right?" I asked.

He nodded.

"That's why Adamistan is so anti-emotion," I said. "Or a big part of it."

"The one below is *Other people feel too much; I feel too little*," Evelyn said, beaming. "I remember you told me that in India, in the field, when we were training in the tuk-tuks. I thought you were full of shit."

"They're connected," I said. "That's why they're next to each other. That day in London, I made a promise to control my emotions, to not let myself feel too much. Over time, that morphed into something even more insidious — *Other people feel too much; I feel too little*. I've said that line a lot in recent years, thinking that belief serves me. It lets me change countries on a whim, attend Vipassana retreats that make me go insane, write vulnerable, personal books about my life and neuroses with the hope they help people feel less crappy about their neuroses. But it has also let me hurt people, like those roaming the desert around Adamistan, because I tell myself other people must function the same way as I do, can repress as I've learned to repress. But they can't. They suffer. Just as I suffer. Just as you suffer when I hide in work and make you feel crazy for constantly showing emotion that I'm not showing, because I've convinced myself I don't possess it. But I do. It's just all stuffed down here. In this weird place. That one's the worse lie of all."

"Don't be melodramatic," Librarian Adam said. "It's both convenient and a truth, that's all."

I pointed. "You suffer," I said. "We don't feel less than other people. If anything, we feel more. We're soft. Sensitive. We eat worms and hide in cupboards and climb out windows. We retreat into the worlds of our head, and those we pour out onto paper. We are masters at suppressing our feelings. But we don't want to be that anymore."

"Please stop," he said, bending forward as if wounded.

"The lies you tell yourself matter as much as the lies you tell other people," I said, and Evelyn nodded, blinking slowly. My eyes filled with tears. Overhead, there was a gurgling sound as a cardboard tube descended from a hole in the ceiling.

"The chute of insight." Librarian Adam beamed. "Hurrah. A new wisdom."

"It's a cardboard tube," I said. It was parcel-taped at various key points. Two new pre-thoughts tumbled out into the fourth filing cabinet, into two unmarked drawers which had opened. Librarian Adam rummaged in his pocket for a pen.

"The wisdom is written on the ball," he explained. "I copy it and then rub it off the bubble, so the memory can be viewed," he said, holding up the first the two bubbles. He turned them in his hand to read the text. "*I don't feel less than other people, I feel more* and *The lies you tell yourself matter just as much as the lies you tell other people.*

Profound wisdoms," he said, writing them onto two strips of tape. "Worthy additions."

He stuck the tape onto the front of the drawer. While his back was to us, I winked at Evelyn.

"Err... is there, like, a place I could interview you?" she asked. "I have some questions about the setup here. Maybe outside? In the warm."

"I haven't been out in many wisdoms," he said.

"It's lovely," she said. "I could show you some... things?"

His eyes darted around. "Hmm."

"I'm just going to sit on this stool," I said, sitting down. "Think about those new wisdoms. What it all means, you know? And I've got a deadline. Maybe do some sentencing."

She reached for his hand; he took it. Slowly, they left. "TOUCH NOTHING!" he shouted over his shoulder.

As soon as they were out of sight, I jumped up and grabbed the two new pre-thoughts, as I was still calling them. Then I went behind the cabinets, where I smashed the glass display case with my elbow and slipped the small brown half-worm into my trouser pocket. In its place, I dropped the pre-thoughts.

Immediately, the cable beneath the stand began to crackle, and great sparks shot in all directions. I took off my T-shirt and held it to the sparks, and when it caught fire, I carried it to the other side of the cabinet, where I began opening drawers and setting the velvet alight. The pre-thoughts proved to be explosive. Beneath me was a distant rumbling, like a volcano waking up. The cabinets were soon a roaring inferno, and I turned and ran for the exit.

I'd just made it out before there was an enormous explosion and the roof of the Great Wisdom Library of Adamistan collapsed.

"What have you done?" Librarian Adam said, as he ran to get back inside. I grabbed him and held him.

"My life's work destroyed!"

"This place is a prison," I said. "I'm setting you free."

"Let me go!"

"Trust me."

"Do not make me hurt you," he said, wriggling a little and then punching me in the stomach.

"Dude, you're eleven. And I know you don't know how to fight because I don't know how to fight. We're only made for running away."

"Run away, then," he said.

I looked him square in the eye. "I know it sucks to be eleven. I know it sucks to have to go to school. I know the world doesn't like you, but it gets better — it gets so much better. And women, my friend. Women are incredible. I'm not saying you'll have many, but the few you will have are spectacular: strong, funny, kooky, smart, not afraid to feel. There is so much good stuff coming."

He stopped fighting me. I let him go. He sat down on the wide top step, wiping away tears with the back of his hand. "You've ruined everything," he said as Evelyn sat down close to him, wrapping her arm around his shoulder.

"No," I said. "Come down to Adamistan with us and you'll see."

At the bottom, I reached for his hand and helped him off the final step. The changes in Adamistan were already obvious. Loud music pulsed — David Hasselhoff's seminal masterpiece *Looking for Freedom* was ringing out at an ear-splitting volume. I remembered a recent documentary I'd seen about the fall of the Berlin Wall. We walked towards the city limits. All around us, Adams hugged, stared into each other's eyes, danced, talked, wept. No one was writing alone or monologuing. The little snatches of conversations we heard were very different, too:

"Tell me about yourself."

"Me? No, I'm not busy."

"Can I help you with that?"

"I love that about you. About all us Adams."

"Those are great trousers. I love the orange tint."

We walked through the crowds towards the plane. At some point, Librarian Adam ran off into the street party. On the section of wall nearest the plane, three Adams stood on the roof of Winnie, our tuk-tuk, knocking at the wall with sledgehammers. A great cheer rang out as the first sizeable chunk gave way. Evelyn and I stood and watched and soon familiar faces, people I'd kicked from my life, were climbing through a narrow gap, entering the city.

When we entered the plane, we found it empty. We sat in the front row. I put the half-worm onto the empty seat next to me.

BING

"Ladies and gentlemen, it's your pilot, Adam Fletcher, here. There's a little commotion here on the ground and so we're going to urgently take off for our flight back to so-called reality. Please close your eyes, relax, and enjoy my competence, which is vast. Thank me."

32

Day 10/10: AM and PM
Location: Bathroom
Mood: Manic pride

After an uneventful ninth day, what had been unimaginable for so long was finally here. I looked at myself in the bathroom mirror. A gaunt face stared back, cheeks hollow. As I cleaned my hands, I thought — reasonably, calmly, slowly, and without mania — *Ain't it funny how time slips away?*

Day ten, day ten, day ten.

The meditation of day nine had been rich and insightful. The sensations had returned. My mind had been calm, and even when it hadn't been, I'd reacted amicably to that change. I had realised something important: my thoughts, whether violent or serene, loud or quiet, focused or scattered, were just as good an object of mindfulness as the breath. This revelation changed everything, meant it was no longer important for my mind to be empty, or for there to be sensations or not. The important thing was what Goenka had been saying all along — being on the bank, not in the stream. I could now answer the question I'd arrived with ten days ago. The question of what I was supposed to feel, learn, or get from meditation:

Meditation and mindfulness are about driving a small gap between stimulus and response, action and reaction, input and output. That might sound trivial, but if the goal is to understand and, to some extent, mitigate your worst impulses, your most harmful misbeliefs and scripts, it's extremely significant.

We have little control over what happens to us, whether as children or as adults. Our only autonomy is in how we react to those things. We are not our thoughts; notions that are often fleeting, hostile, contradictory, and violent, as I had experienced so excruciatingly here.

When we're mindful while hovering our flip-flop over scurrying ants or watching a man cut the core of our apple, or before throwing wine at people in Spanish-themed restaurants or answering a plea for help with the word *nope*, we can pause, just briefly, and notice how we're responding, notice where our mind is going and whether we want to follow it there — to a place of self-doubt, hatred, petty vengeance, or even shallow, narcissistic glory. A place like Adamistan.

The terrain of meditation was rich and vast and I had only just started exploring it, but I had a lifetime for that. I felt my impermanence strongly. Knew that I had arisen and would one day pass away. I didn't want to be at the retreat anymore. I wanted to be with her. I wanted to be out in the world doing, feeling, experiencing, loving, unbalancing my mind in as many interesting ways as possible. Life is more interesting not when you have control, but when you surrender it.

So after the first few sessions, I found YoungUriGellar by the canteen. "I know you said no one is allowed to leave on the tenth day, but I want to leave."

"That's not possible," he said.

"I can't do another minute of meditation. I have a pregnant girlfriend I want to get back to. She might need me. I need her."

His nose scrunched. "Let me talk to the course leader, okay?"

33

A few minutes later, YoungUriGellar led me to a small office next to the meditation hall for a private meeting with Penfold. He was sitting at a pine desk. It was jarring to see him sitting on an office chair and surrounded by documents, like some kind of spiritual middle manager.

He gestured to an empty chair, its back to the wall. It squeaked as I sat. I felt like a naughty child called to see the headteacher.

"I hear you would like to leave?" he said. His voice was flat and dull, like German fields.

"Do we have only three minutes?" I asked, looking around for the tiny bell. My words came out heavy and misshapen, like dented tins. I was shocked by how quickly you could forget how to do something you'd taken for granted.

"No," he said, glancing towards the door. "We have as long as you need."

I relaxed into my chair and cleared my throat. "I feel I've got a lot of benefits from my time here but that I'm done now."

"I understand," he said, calmly, because apparently

everyone who worked here had to be insufferably calm all the time.

I wanted to grab them all by their collars and shake them and shout, "EMOTION IS NOT THE ENEMY. IGNORANCE IS THE ENEMY. INDIFFERENCE IS THE ENEMY."

"You committed to staying until the end," he continued.

"I know. And it is the end."

"Tomorrow is the end."

"It's basically the end."

He raised his hands from his lap in a defensive gesture. "I'd ask you to trust me. It's really important you don't leave today. It's a group experience that we started, and it works only if the entire group finishes it."

"But other people have left already. Loads of them."

"Some, yes. But not near the end. If you leave today, others will start having doubts and it will snowball from there. Goenka called this the stop-brake day for a reason. All this stuff has come up while you've been here, and it needs time to settle before you're ready to go back out into the world."

"It has settled," I said. "I need to get back to my life."

He hesitated. "Why is it you think you can't stay?"

"I can't do any more meditation. I just don't believe in it. Well, I mean, I believe in it. I just don't believe it's the best thing for me right now. And I'm having difficulties with Goenka. I've always had difficulties with him. How he claims not to be a guru but acts so exactly like a guru."

"I understand."

"The problem is not *what* you're teaching," I said, my voice thick with self-righteousness, "but *how* you're teaching it. Can I ask you a personal question?"

"Sure."

"Do you ever have doubts about the way the technique is being taught?"

He blinked heavily then looked away, that wide, self-satisfied grin falling from his face. "Yes," he said, finally. "But it's a... kind of package. It's designed to help the most people possible. I think it does that." He nodded, happy with his answer. "Whatever you're making the object of your aversion — the course, Goenka, meditation, me, it can be anything, because it's not about that thing — you're deciding to feel that about it, to identify with those negative sensations."

"I know."

"So, don't. You don't have to meditate if you don't want to. You can just sit quietly in the back and explore your saṅkhāras, see what aversions are sitting behind them."

I groaned. "You can't just reduce everything to a saṅkhāra of craving or aversion. It's too simplistic. It's disrespectful, almost. We're not worms."

He looked confused, and I realised why. It was the same problem I'd had several times in the past days: he was not in my head. The experiences I'd had during this retreat were so intense, it was hard for me to remember that they'd happened only to me, mostly inside the various layers of my mind.

I straightened. "At some point it has to be legitimate for a person to say, 'I've carefully considered something for a long period of time, during which, mostly, my mind was equanimous, and I've concluded that it's not good for me'. Why can't I have a rationally created preference? Goenka's way can't be the only way."

He sighed. "But in life, there are so many situations where we can't choose to leave and must simply endure, correct?"

I smiled. He didn't know how much effort I'd put into

creating the exact opposite of that life. And how successful I'd been at it. Only now, only because of this experience, did I understand what that had cost me and the people around me.

"That's what the technique helps you with," he said, when I didn't answer because I was busy thinking and looking over his shoulder out the window. It had been a long time since I'd had a conversation; I was rusty.

"Soon you will be back out in the world, and there you'll see how much everything you've learned here helps you," he said, pumped up with certainty. "Keep enduring. If you want to, see Goenka as being designed specifically to provoke a reaction from you. Decide he's actively trying to unbalance your mind."

I laughed. "He's pretty good at it."

Penfold smiled. "And your challenge is to not let him."

Somehow, it had never dawned on me that maybe, just maybe, Goenka was deliberately being this irritating and repetitive to challenge our equanimity; I would not let Goenka defeat me.

Spite. Here it was again.

"Okay," I said. "I'll stay, I guess. I can write now anyway, right? And we can talk after lunch?"

He looked up at the clock. "The rules change at midday, yes."

It was three minutes to twelve. Writing. I'd missed it even more than talking.

I thanked him and ran to my locker in the canteen, where I retrieved my notepad and pen, which, perhaps melodramatically, I kissed. I had so much stuff I'd been carrying in my head — ideas, phrases, jokes, stories, sentences, so many things I wanted to tell Evelyn, myself, you.

I spread open the notepad on a table in the canteen and

poured out everything I could remember — Freddie, Apple-FuckFace, the worm, Sarah, the threesome, Adamistan.

My head had been so heavy. The thoughts needed to be set free.

In a thirty-minute frenzy, I emptied it all onto paper. Each day, its number marked in the top-left corner of the page, became several pages. When it was over, when the surging wave of words had receded, I leaned back in my chair and looked at the inky scrawl, my handwriting no better than when I'd been in middle school. Then I burst into tears, as per usual. Just the latest outburst of an emotional man. Around me were other men and I should have cared, but I didn't. I was so full of gratitude that this was my job, that I was neither a worm nor younger me in the playground being forced to eat the worm. I thought of Evelyn and how I wouldn't be here without her, wouldn't have learned all this without her pushing back against my worst tendencies.

A stranger offered me a tissue. It broke the spell and I looked up and around — I was the only person writing. I stopped writing. There would be time for this later. First, something else I had missed. People. One in particular. His name was Freddie.

34

I slid open the door to the back terrace. A scary large ginger face jumped into my path.

"How was it?" GingerCircusBear asked, and I wondered if my eyes were glowing like his now that I was in on the secret. In the club. One of his people.

"'Horrendous," I said. "Why didn't you warn me?"

"You wouldn't have believed me. No one who hasn't done one of these would."

"I'll try to make them," I said. "But no, I wouldn't have believed you. And you? How was your fifth?"

He took a deep breath that seemed to wind him. "It's just a batshit-crazy process, isn't it? A lot of different stuff came up. New demons. I went to some dark places. My body handled it fine, but there were so many sessions where my mind was just screaming at me to flee."

"Yeah," I said. "I hear you. And a sixth?"

"For sure. And I'm not going to wait two years until the next one, either. You?"

"NEVER AGAIN."

We laughed.

"Let's see," he said, as I excused myself to go find Freddie. It's a weird thing to share a room with someone during such an intense experience, to hear them howling and sobbing and having their guts pulled up through their throat and out their mouth and yet not offer them any consolation. We had both haunted our room and each other. I felt extremely close to him, yet he knew nothing about me. He was holding court at the back of the terrace, near the low fence I'd climbed on day four, when so much had happened. He looked happy to have an audience again.

"What a ride, huh, boys? I feel like I went to war, only both sides were me. Know what I mean? Of course you do. Did we win? I don't know. But we made it and that has to mean something, right?" He lifted his chin. "We leave here as conquerors."

A few of his small audience cheered. He spotted me and came over and we hugged awkwardly until YoungUri-Gellar appeared, to remind us that there was to be no physical contact today.

"One second," I said to Freddie, then gestured Young-UriGellar to follow me. We took a few steps away from the group. I tried to remember which day I'd told him about AppleFuckFace, but they'd all blurred somewhat. "What happened to the two people who were talking?" I asked.

His eyes circled in thought. I wondered how many people had been caught talking.

"I think it was day four or five," I added. "Near the accommodation block for returning meditators?"

"I remember," he said. "I found them talking. I told them I'd need to discuss their punishment with the course leaders. They got angry about that and quit."

I hadn't been punished for trying to leave. "Do you punish here?"

"Rarely. Especially if there are mitigating circumstances," he said, and we both knew what he was hinting at.

Only I knew, however, that they actually hadn't been mitigating at all. Shame arose. I waited to see how long it would last.

"Sorry again about your grandfather," he said.

I went back to Freddie, who was sitting at the end of a long bench. I slid onto the long bench, opposite him.

"So, you made it," he said, smiling. "And you better believe I had my doubts."

"You made it too. Well done, buddy."

He brushed his hair forward with his hand. "It was close, though," he said, lowering his voice. "I had such a torrid time."

"Tell me about it." I said, but he would have told me about it anyway.

"Well," he began, and I settled in for a monologue of indeterminate length. "I went insane. I was just a lunatic. I actually head-butted a tree." He touched a wound on his forehead. "Who head-butts a tree? What did the tree do wrong? It's just... I couldn't get away. Couldn't get out. It's like every person I hurt, every stupid thing I said, every wife I lost, every moment I failed — all these things threw a party with me in the middle, strapped to a table. They took turns to come up, to come inches from my face, and they laughed at me. All of them. It lasted centuries."

I nodded sympathetically.

"It was a bleak, bleak experience," he continued. "On the fourth day, I woke up in tears and went to Kevin."

"The course leader?" I asked, assuming he meant Penfold.

"Yeah. And I said, 'This technique seems to work, Kevin, all this stuff is coming up. But *how* does it work?' And Kevin tried to tell me a Goenka fable about burning logs. I stopped him halfway through. 'YEAH, BUT HOW DOES IT WORK, KEVIN?' He took one of those long breaths. 'We don't really know', he said. 'Just that it works'."

"It sure does," the man next to me said.

"Goenka fables are the worst," I added.

"Less Goenka and a bit more meditation would have been better," said Freddie. I rocked backwards in horror. "Steady on there," he said. "No one said anything about more meditation."

"Did you get some answers, though?" I asked Freddie.

"About?"

"What to do next? Your marriages? Your neighbours? Your job? Your dog?"

"I'm going on my trip and I'm not coming back."

"Good for you."

"And you?" he asked.

"Never again," I said, my new mantra.

"Really?" interrupted a middle-aged Austrian. "For me, ten days wasn't enough." He was on his tenth Vipassana. "The most important thing for you all now," he said, authoritatively, making eye contact with us both, "is to stay with the program. Do as Goenka says — two hours of meditation a day."

"Two hours!" I scoffed. "Who has a spare two hours?" Once I had a baby, I'd probably struggle to find a spare twenty minutes.

"Anyone who wants a balanced mind," he said, and I believed him, but it didn't matter, because I didn't want a balanced mind. What I wanted, they didn't have at this place.

It was almost time to go find her.

35

The next morning, after helping to clean the retreat and making a generous donation so that others could come and have this extraordinary, soul-quaking experience, I put my rucksack next to the gate and waited for the minibus, thinking about how many hours I'd spent imagining this exact moment, not believing I'd ever reach it.

I was insanely proud of myself.

The ten-day Vipassana had been a serious mental undertaking. This wasn't something someone should bluster into. It had been wrong of Evelyn to send me here, although she'd done it for the right reasons. And anyway, from wrong decisions, you can still reach right answers. I felt as if I'd only just escaped with my sanity. There was a lot of work for me to do now, but I didn't see how that work could be harder than what I'd already done here.

I took a deep breath and turned on my phone. Once the shower of messages and notifications passed, I wrote Evelyn. She had sent me one photo each day since day four — each day, a photo of a different positive pregnancy test.

> Adam: No matter what I tell you, no matter how I spin it, present it, justify it, never ever ever ever ever ever ever ever ever ever ever ever ever ever ever ever let me do a Vipassana again.
>
> Evelyn: That good?

The train took a frustratingly long time to reach Berlin, a dirty, stinking, sexy Mecca of unbridled hedonism. I wanted to indulge. To play the game of sensations — not patiently and persistently but impatiently and whimsically.

Most of all, I wanted her.

No, I craved her.

I needed to tell her all the ways she mattered to me. How wrong I'd been about myself and about how I'd handled the past year. IVF and the looming spectre of infertility had nearly broken us, as it did many couples. I hadn't understood what had happened to her, how her mind had snapped until mine did here. But she was pregnant now. And I had much self-knowledge. I would use the techniques of Vipassana and mindfulness to interrupt the automatic scripts my mind followed. We had a second chance, she and I. In nine months, we would be parents.

I ran from the subway station, clutching my now well-worn cushions and mats in my big blue IKEA bag. And then there it was, our grey door.

Our stairs.

Many, many stairs. Had there always been so many stairs? Had someone added new stairs? I should have been fit. I'd done so much walking. I didn't seem to be fit.

Second floor.

Third floor.

Fourth floor.

I reached for my keys, but she'd already heard me coming. She claimed she always knew my footsteps on the stairs. That there was something distinctive about them. The door flew open and we smashed into each other and swirled ungracefully and fell against the wall. I banged my head on the key cupboard.

"I missed you," I said, plunging my face into her hair and breathing in that scent — the tropics. A holiday. Yes, we could use all that money we'd save by avoiding the final two IVF nukes to get out of this place, to go where the memories would be as fresh as the coconuts.

"Are you still with child?" I asked. The answer was obvious. She was beaming, glowing as I'd felt I was glowing around day seven.

"Did a test an hour ago," she said. "Nothing faint about the line, I can tell you. It's an expensive hobby, being pregnant. But it's different this time. Feels different."

"Can't be more expensive than trying to become pregnant," I said, as I lifted her from her feet and we waddled to the bedroom and I tried to throw her but mostly just dropped her onto the bed while kicking a box. I stopped. "That the success box?"

"Yep."

"What's in it?"

"Not worth the wait," she said, as I pulled off my jumper.

"This will be," I said.

"Any major life changes?" she asked, grabbing my hands, trying to slow me down as I reached for her clothes. A mirror of the scene where she'd tried to rush me because she was ovulating. "I was afraid you'd come out, take a vow of celibacy, and go live the rest of your days in a hut."

"Celibacy?" I howled with laughter and wrestled her hands and ripped at her clothes and we had wonderful, destabilising, intense sex — full of saṅkhāras of craving. I loved every one of them, just as I loved her.

"That retreat was the hardest thing I've ever done," I said, when we'd finished and lay sweaty, her hair tickling my cheek, staring up at the mites of dust twirling in the gorgeous mid-afternoon light streaming in through the windows; I ran my finger slowly up her arm.

"What?" she asked. "Harder than the last year and a half? Than infertility?"

"Yes," I said, without hesitation. "A hundred times, yes. There was nowhere to hide there."

"Wow," she said, staring up at me, seemingly trying to imagine that. It should have been easy to imagine. She'd been to the same place, had been a confused, scared custodian of a malfunctioning mind.

"But I also learned an incredible amount," I said. "It was like a thousand hours of therapy. Even so, you shouldn't have sent me there." I told her about the worm. About her threesome. About Adamistan. "I don't regret it," I said. "And you were right. It's possible for someone to know you better than you know yourself, but only if you're not actually trying to know yourself, which I wasn't."

"I also did things I'm not proud of," she said. "I think I was also trying to push you away by the end. I made us suffer more than we had to."

"I should have done more," I said. "I just didn't understand."

"Maybe."

"Anyway," I said, "being a parent can't be harder than infertility, right?"

It took quite some time for the laughter to die down.

36

Four months after the retreat

I was standing in what would become our child's bedroom, in what had been Evelyn's room, the room of so many of my disturbed erotic fantasies during the retreat. There was a drill in my hand and a frown born of intense confusion on my face. Evelyn had offered to help, but I felt it was important that I do this alone. That she shouldn't be the only person in the house who knew how to use power tools.

I squinted at the idiotic instructions for assembling a chest of drawers and a changing table that was supposed to attach, somehow, to its top and then to the wall. It might as well have been in Mandarin. Then I picked up a piece of wood that was 3a or perhaps 7b and, maturely, threw it against the wall and screamed.

A voice spoke to me. It was Goenka's.

"Annoyance has arisen," it said.

"Oh, goodie. Let's see how long it lasts."

I took a deep, calming breath.

In... left nostril.
Out... both nostrils.

Where did the feeling sit, I wondered? I followed it down to the base of my throat. What shape did it have? It was... jagged. No, star shaped? I held it as an entomologist might a rare butterfly. Did I want to play its game of sensations?

No.

I had work to do, and annoyance wasn't going to help me do it. I had long ago decided I was bad at building things, that my mind wasn't structured and systematic, as other men's seemed to be, but that belief wasn't serving me. Was wrong. Stupid. I could do this. It was just adult Lego.

I just had to accept that I didn't know better than the instructions. That they should lead and I should follow. I picked up the wood, flipped the instructions back to the first page.

"Is the paint even dry?" Evelyn asked, appearing at the doorway in her dressing gown, rubbing at the small bump under it, a compulsion she'd developed — that and taking pregnancy tests. Our bins were always full of them.

I looked around at the ocean blue we'd spent the morning applying to the walls. "Dry enough," I said, marking an X on the wall.

"I can't believe you bought that already," she said, looking at the scattered pieces of what would become the changing table all over the wooden floor. "It's too soon."

"I'm nesting."

She smiled. "I see that."

"Step back, my love. I'm about to teach this wall a lesson."

"Make it quick. We've got the scan soon."

. . .

An hour later, we emerged from the subway for my first visit to Evelyn's gynaecologist. As we sat in the waiting room, I swam back through assorted memories of the fertility clinic, not quite able to believe we'd never need to go to that horrid place again. They had the same poster here — "The Miracle of Life."

"I bet you miss the Masturbatorium, right?" she joked.

"I should download *Lesbian Vampire Academy* for us."

She patted my hand. "I'm good, thanks."

"I'm kind of curious about how it ends."

"Should we send them something?" she asked. "Like, as a thank you?"

"The Vampire Academy?"

"The clinic, of course."

"We paid that monster bill. Wasn't that nice enough of us?"

"Worth every penny."

A woman called Evelyn's name and then we were in a room and Evelyn lay down, bump exposed. I squeezed her clammy hand and we grinned at each other and I realised that this was one of those moments.

A rite.

A ritual.

A marker on a path new for her and me but well-trodden by a wider Us. Just as I'd been trying to catch up with the other meditators, who'd surely been racing ahead of me towards enlightenment, Evelyn and I were now catching up with the parents of lust babies for which — not primed to expect everything to always go wrong — moments like this were more joyous than terrifying.

The doctor lathered magic jelly across Evelyn's bump and rubbed at it with a special dildo.

It started with a sound.

Fast.

Rapid.

BOOM BOOM BOOM BOOM BOOM BOOM BOOM BOOM BOOM

Should it be that fast? Was mine that fast once?

"A beautiful heartbeat," the doctor said, in German, and I laughed at the memory of the doctor who thought he'd permanently changed Evelyn's language centre.

Lines on the monitor. The doctor turned a dial and there was a picture, a blizzard cutting in and out as she moved the paddle across Evelyn's womb. That blizzard reminded me of Ghost Evelyn, cutting in and out of my memories. In the centre of the storm, a gummy bear. No, a tadpole.

"And look at that heart," the doctor said, appreciatively, as if seeing art for which she had long thirsted. "That's a beautiful heart. And we should be able to... If we just... There we... Yes, a girl," she said, sitting forward in her chair. "Ninety percent sure."

I burst into tears. We'd have a lot more names to pick from.

The doctor stopped. Turned to me. "You okay?"

"No," I said. "But that's fine. Carry on."

I pulled a pack of tissues from my pocket. Evelyn was crying too, gripping my hand as if she were trying to wrench it off. I lifted it and kissed her knuckles. Everything was fine. Better than fine. Our picture-postcard-perfect embryo was becoming a picture-postcard-perfect daughter.

"You okay getting home?" I asked Evelyn, when we were back on the street, people passing us, each one once a blob on a snow-filled screen observed by grinning parents clutching each other's clammy hands.

She made her *Really?* face at my question. "How pregnant do you think I am?"

"Okay," I said. "I won't be home late."

"Bring food," she said, and descended into the mouth of the subway.

Another waiting room. The furniture expensive. Scandinavian. No posters, just paintings —originals featuring abstract bright swirls I decided were supposed to suggest mountain vistas and running streams and sturdy people flourishing in nature. Just me waiting.

A door slid open.

"Adam," said a smartly dressed, well-groomed man in his forties. He reminded me a little of Penfold, the designer edition. "Welcome."

I went in. Sat. Scanned my body, sweeping from top to bottom. What feelings were there? What sensations? Which did I want to identify with?

Excitement.

"What are you hoping to explore here?" my new therapist asked.

"I want to be better at loving people," I said, and didn't even smirk. There's no shame in needing a little help. Some things don't arise to pass away. They fester within your subconscious, sitting so long and so deep that you don't even know that they're there, that they're changing how you see the world, move through the world, and, in turn, how the world reacts to you. I would keep trying to reach them, understand them, challenge them, bring them to the surface — with Evelyn, with friends, through honest writing like this, through meditation, through therapy, and in discussions with my daughter.

He nodded, slightly. "Let's start at the beginning. Tell me about your family," he said. "About your childhood."

"My childhood?" I said, relaxing into his expensively upholstered chair. "Ain't it funny how time slips away?"

THE END

* * *

Thank you for reading. Without you, there would be no books.

Would you like there to be more of them? Do you want to know what happened next in my life? The easiest way to show me that is to leave a rating, review, or tell a friend about this book. There is so much more I want to write about.

Until then,

Adam

PS: You can also get an exclusive free book, *Lost But Not Least*, at adam-fletcher.co.uk

ALSO BY ADAM FLETCHER

- Non-fiction -

Don't Go There (Weird Travel Series #1)

Don't Come Back (Weird Travel Series #2 and Writer's Digest Memoir of the year winner)

Tuk-tuk for Two (Weird Travel Series #3)

After Happy Ever After (Weird Travel Series #4)

Lost But Not Least (an exclusive free book for my newsletter subscribers)

Understanding the British

Fast Philosophy

- Fiction (as Adam R. Fletcher) -

The Death of James Jones, sort of

Printed in Great Britain
by Amazon